World Religions

World Religions

S.A. NIGOSIAN

Edward Arnold

Original edition © Copp Clark Publishing 1974
This edition © Edward Arnold (Publishers) Ltd 1975

This edition first published 1975
by Edward Arnold (Publishers) Ltd
41 Bedford Square, London WC1B 3DQ
Reprinted 1978, 1981, 1982

ISBN: 0 7131 0008 7

Short extracts from translations of various sacred texts
are acknowledged as follows:

Charles Scribner's Sons,
>   E. Hume, *The World's Living Religions.*

Harper & Row Publishers, Inc.,
>   S. Nikhilananda, *The Upanishads.*
>   F. Edgerton, *The Bhagavdad Gita.*

Oxford University Press,
>   A. J. Arberry, *The Koran Interpreted.*

Thomas Nelson & Sons,
>   *The Holy Bible* (Revised Standard Version).

Washington Square Press, Inc.,
>   G. Brantl, *Catholicism.*
>   J. A. Williams, *Islam.*
>   L. Renou, *Hinduism.*
>   A. Hertzberg, *Judaism.*

Jehangir B. Karani's Sons,
>   J. J. Modi, *The Naojote Ceremony of the Parsees.*

Printed in Great Britain by
Whitstable Litho Ltd., Whitstable, Kent

Contents

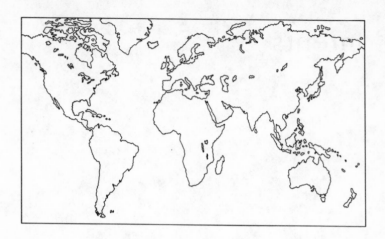

Name of Religion	Country of Origin	Name & Date of Founder	Scripture	Distribution
Hinduism	India	Rishis (1500 B.C.)	Vedas	India
Buddhism	India	Gautama – The Buddha (563 – 483 B.C.)	Tripitakas	India, Ceylon, Thailand, Mongolia, Manchuria, Tibet, China, Korea and Japan. Adherents also found in Europe, Britain and North America.
Taoism	China	Li-Poh Yang (Lao-Tzu) (±570 – ? B.C.)	Tao-Te-Ching	China
Confucianism	China	K'ung-Fu-Tzu (551 – 479 B.C.)	The Classics	China
Shintoism	Japan	Prehistoric	Ko-Jiki Nihon-Shoki	Japan
Zoroastrianism (Parseeism)	Persia	Zarathustra (628 – 551 B.C.)	Avesta	Persia and India.
Judaism	Palestine	Moses (Date unknown; ? 14th Cent. B.C.)	The Bible (Old Testament)	Israel and throughout the world.
Christianity	Palestine	Jesus – The Christ (4 B.C. – A.D. 29)	The Bible (Old & New Testament)	North & South America, Britain, Europe, U.S.S.R., Australia. Adherents also found all over the world.
Islam	Arabia	Mohammed (c.a. 571 – 632 A.D.)	Qur'an	Turkey, Africa, Iran, India, China. Adherents also found all over the world.

Preface

This book is deliberately limited and selective in concept. Its purpose is to present concisely, in terms of modern times, a picture of six of the more important living religions; and, in doing that, to offer an invitation and a key to deeper study of this vast and absorbing aspect of man's nature. The emphasis is on issues that bring men together rather than dividing them, and for each religion I have restricted myself to common ground shared by most of its adherents.

At the opening, three important themes are presented in outline. The first of these is the change in traditional, moral, and religious values that has been caused by the progress of science and technology. Then, the word "religion" and the problems that are encountered in attempting to define it are discussed. This is followed by some consideration of the advantages and disadvantages of a "universal" religion, as against a "mosaic" of religions. The main chapters of Judaism, Christianity, Islam, Hinduism, Buddhism, and Zoroastrianism follow next, in that order, which, from the viewpoint of readers from the Judaic and Christian traditions, moves from the more familiar to the less familiar areas of religious tradition.

For each of the six religions that I deal with, the reader will find a geographical and historical survey, a description of the founder or teacher, a review of the sacred writings or literature, a discussion of the central concepts and philosophical views, a description of the more important practices and ceremonies, and an indication of the various denominations and institutions. Extensive use is made of excerpts from the sacred writings of each religion. A comparative chart, a glossary, and numerous photographs are provided to help the reader, and the bibliography points the way to deeper study through the complete texts of sacred works and through other books on religion.

Bygone and tribal religions have been purposely omitted in favour of a more detailed study of six major surviving religions. For books dealing with these and other aspects of religion that are not within the scope of this book, or are dealt with only briefly, the reader is referred to the bibliography.

I want to acknowledge a debt of gratitude to all who have inspired and stimulated my thinking through the years, but I will mention here only those who have been directly concerned with this volume: my three colleagues, Professors Sol Tanenzapf and Kazumaro Fujimoto, who gave me the benefit of their discerning criticism, and Professor Jordan Paper, who made numerous suggestions for improving the manuscript; Patrick Trant, Christine Yaworsky, and Tom Fairley of Copp Clark Publishing for their constant encouragement and painstaking editorial work; Debbie van Eeken, who assisted in sorting out various pertinent information; my two efficient secretaries, Molly Klein and Mrs. Nancy Enright, who, with their skill and patience, were most helpful in the preparation of this book.

Without the support and understanding of my wife and our two children, my efforts would have been in vain; this volume is dedicated to them, not out of sentimentality, but with a deep sense of gratitude and affection.

S.A.N.

INTRODUCTION

> The need of the moment is not one religion, but mutual respect and tolerance of the devotees of the different religions. We want to reach not dead level, but unity in diversity. The soul of religions is one, but it is encased in a multitude of forms. The latter will persist to the end of time.
>
> Mahatma Gandhi

When he referred to the "soul of religions" Gandhi meant man's universal quest for truth, peace and goodness. By "a multitude of forms" he meant the many ways in which man expresses his beliefs and attitudes.

No matter when or how man developed, from the time he became man his irresistible urge to worship has created, and still creates, endless forms of religious behaviour. Indeed, so powerful is this force within man that it has produced a mosaic of beliefs, attitudes, and practices. Yet there is a unity within this rich diversity.

Surrounded and often threatened by forces which he seldom understood, man has sought to penetrate the mystery of life. No matter when or where he has lived, man's religious needs have not changed: to bear the sorrows of life man needs strength; to face the daily battle for survival he needs protection; in the hour of conflict he needs assurance; in the hour of grief he needs comfort. To soothe the pangs of conscience man needs a faith; to face the dangers of life he needs a conviction; to break the grip of fear and loneliness he needs sustaining courage.

To find a way to live peacefully in spite of forces which tend to thrust man into destructive conflict is only one aspect of man's search. The other aspect is his eternal quest for a purpose in his existence. Both are legitimate goals for man: to look for ways of avoiding or escaping dangers that threaten his life, on the one hand; and to look for inspiration, or a profound motivation to justify his existence, on the other. These two goals are inseparable and together they represent the ultimate goal of all religions; they will remain so to the end of time.

The record of man's faith from the earliest times is beyond the scope of this book. Besides, many religions rose only to disappear quickly, leaving little or no trace. Others flourished only as long as a particular civilization or nation flourished, but died with it. A few, however, were destined to persist as living religions to the present era. But even these few are being profoundly affected by the revolutionary changes of modern times.

The achievements of science and technology have radically altered the pattern of man's life: socially, economically, politically, and intellectually. The same changes are also affecting his moral and religious values.

Man has been so successful in breaking the bonds of gravity and reaching the moon that he can look at the universe and his position in it from a new perspective. His progress in explaining "natural" causes and effects has eliminated his fear and awe of "supernatural" phenomena. His medical achievements have advanced to the point where healing can be explained without dependence on superstitious beliefs and magical rites.

A parallel development is profoundly affecting the values and traditions of the major religions. Both adults and young people are experiencing what is known as an "identity crisis". This simply means that man is still involved in the eternal quest: his identity in this universe; the true meaning or purpose of his existence.

Religious beliefs are either being questioned or discarded as inadequate and obsolete. But there is nothing new in this. Centuries ago some of the religious geniuses, such as Moses, Jesus, Mohammed, Buddha, and Zoroaster faced similar struggles. The solutions they proposed influenced the lives of millions and shaped the endless forms of the major living religions.

For this reason alone these religions merit our attention and especially our respectful understanding so that we may appreciate the values that each has brought to the millions who have accepted them. It is only too easy to laugh or to sneer at unfamiliar ideas and customs. Such words as "pagan", "idolatry", "heathen", and "superstition" should not be part of our vocabulary. They are usually derogatory terms to describe someone else's beliefs, seldom our own. An objective study demands sympathetic understanding.

"Religion" and "religious" are terms which appear self-explanatory, yet defy precise definition because they carry different meanings for different people.

To define "religious" in terms of adherence to a particular faith or participation in a particular form of worship simply excludes all those outside that faith as well as all those within the faith who do not share a particular viewpoint or way of expressing it. On the other hand, to define the term religious in its classical sense, as a characteristic of people who believe in a god, is also inadequate, because this definition excludes all those who act and behave very much like conventional religious believers although they may not, like the Buddhists, believe in a god.

To say that one is religious when one *thinks about* a god is to commit the error of restricting the meaning to *intellectual* activity. On the other hand, to say that one is religious when one *feels* an experience is to restrict the meaning to *emotional* activity. Man is a being with multiple capacities; he thinks, feels, and acts by responding inwardly as well as outwardly.

It seems a mistake to define religion very narrowly, but it is dangerous to define it so broadly that the term loses all significance. For instance, to say that religion is "awe" or "wonder" or "love" is to say little, because a flash of lightning or a flight of birds can inspire awe or wonder, and love is as often equated with self-indulgence or self-gratification as it is with self-sacrifice. Awe, wonder, and love are only aspects of religion.

It is also misleading to think of religion as a code of ethics or of morals since there are people who can reject all religions and still maintain high moral and ethical standards. Belief in a religion or loyalty to a particular faith is no guarantee against immoral or unethical behaviour. The pages of human history are filled with accounts of "religious" people who have committed "immoral" acts, often in the name of their religions.

The man who estimated that there were ten thousand definitions of religion probably understated the case. Of course it is impossible to examine all ten thousand definitions but it is useful to cite a few examples in order to indicate the range of opinion.

Some definitions emphasize the intellectual function of religion:

> Religion is a mental faculty or disposition which, independent of sense or reason, enables man to apprehend the Infinite under different names and under varying guises.
>
> Max Muller

Some explanations stress the emotional function:

> The essence of religion is the feeling of absolute dependence.
>
> Schleiermacher

Others express the worship function:

> Religion is the worship of higher powers from the sense of need.
>
> Allan Menzies

Still others relate religion to individual experiences:

> Religion . . . shall mean for us, the feelings, acts and experiences of individual men in their solitude, so far as they apprehend themselves to stand in relation to whatever they consider the divine.
>
> William James

Yet another viewpoint emphasizes the social function of religion:

> Religion is the consciousness of the highest social values.
>
> Edward S. Ames

Naturally, most definitions of religion are satisfactory up to a point. We might expect to find the most inclusive statement about religion in a dictionary, so why not turn to the Merriam Webster *New International Dictionary* to seek an explanation:

> Religion . . . is the outward act or form by which men indicate their recognition of the existence of a god or of gods having power over their destiny, to whom obedience, service, and honour are due; the feeling or expression of human love, fear, or awe of some superhuman and over-ruling power, whether by profession of belief, by observance of rites and ceremonies, or by the conduct of life.

This definition seems broad enough to explain religion in terms of worship, of belief, of feeling, and of conduct. Is it good enough? Does it suggest a need for further elaboration?

No one, for instance, can study themes of art or forms of architecture without some reference to the impetus provided by religion. Similarly, one cannot learn about music and poetry without somehow mentioning the influence of religious inspiration. Neither history, nor sociology, nor anthropology can be taught or interpreted without consideration of religious customs and practices. To discuss psychology without reference to religion as a force which motivates, regulates, influences, and even directs the behaviour of many individuals is almost impossible. What is true of these few disciplines is also true to a greater or a lesser degree of politics, economics, philosophy, medicine, and so on.

Most of these definitions fall into two general categories: one category of definition seeks to explain *what* religion is by analysing man's attitudes and behaviour, while the other seeks to explain *why* religion is a factor in human affairs by analysing the motives behind man's attitudes and behaviour. But what sort of human attitudes and behaviour are to be regarded as "religious"?

Opinions differ so widely that an intelligent answer is impossible without some knowledge about the history of religion and how different people act when they are religious. Needless to say, this kind of answer depends on an appreciation for the values which each individual religion gives to its followers and a sympathetic understanding of how people in different times and under different circumstances thought, felt, and behaved. Moreover, in the light of modern psychology, it is the differences and not the similarities that make life interesting and enrich one's experience and awareness. So let us explore the many facets of the major living religions of our time.

A quotation which seems particularly appropriate as a concluding statement to this introduction comes from a great contemporary Hindu philosopher, and the former president of the Republic of India, S. Radhakrishnan:

> ... Believers with different opinions and convictions are necessary to each other . . . We cannot afford to waver in our determination that the whole of Humanity shall remain a united people, where Moslem and Christian, Buddhist and Hindu shall stand together, bound by a common devotion not to something behind but to something ahead, not to a racial past or a geographical unit, but to a great dream of a world society with a universal religion of which the historical faiths are but branches.
>
> Radhakrishnan

JUDAISM

The Menorah:
Symbol of religious liberty

Hear, O Israel: the Lord our God is one Lord; and you shall love the Lord your God with all your heart, and with all your soul, and with all your might. And these words which I command you this day shall be upon your heart; and you shall teach them diligently to your children, and shall talk of them when you sit in your house, and when you walk by the way, and when you lie down, and when you rise. And you shall bind them as a sign upon your hand, and they shall be as frontlets between your eyes. And you shall write them on the doorposts of your house and on your gates.

Deuteronomy 6:4-9

JUDAISM

The early records of the religious history of Judaism, as well as of Christianity and Islam, date from the classical period of the "ancient Israelites", sometimes referred to as "early Hebrews", a Semitic group which roamed the northern Arabian desert. Just as other nomadic groups lived in tribes with a chieftain in authority over its members, so around the second millenium B.C. the patriarch Abraham and his people lived and travelled on the fringes of the desert seeking pasture for their animals (Genesis 12-25). They normally encamped beside springs and oases, but because vegetation was sparse they had to be on the move continuously. Crossing and recrossing desert wastes of pebbles and shifting sand, they travelled in search of fruit, vegetation, and water.

For centuries at a time, they lived in perfect freedom. But, some five hundred years after the time of Abraham, the Hebrew people found themselves enslaved in order to provide labour for the rich and splendid civilization of the Pharaohs in Egypt. Soon, however, a great deliverer was to appear who would lead the Hebrew people to the promised land.

About 1,300 years before the Christian era, the enslaved tribes, under the leadership of Moses, broke out of Egypt and made their way into the cultivated land of Canaan – the area which lies between the Jordan River and the Mediterranean Sea. A bloody struggle followed between the Canaanite inhabitants and the Hebrew immigrants, lasting for some three hundred years, until David succeeded temporarily in uniting the two groups. Less than a hundred years later, the kingdom of Israel was split into two independent states: the larger northern state known as Israel, and the smaller southern state known as Judah. Within four hundred years, both states were engulfed by the powerful Assyrian and Babylonian empires. Except for the short Hasmonean period (142-63 B.C.), the Jewish people never again enjoyed political independence until the present century; in the interval, they learned to live in dispersion, adhering to their social customs and religious traditions.

For the Jewish people, historical events are far more than a mere sequence of names and incidents; to them, historical events are acts of a god who is deliberately and purposefully guiding his people onwards. Jewish people therefore see all historical events as crucial to the formation of their religion; in order to understand the character of Judaism, we have to examine its history.

The Bible

The Hebrew Bible provides a good starting point for this examination. The term "Bible" is derived from a Greek word which means "books"; both Jews and Christians use the term Bible to mean the sacred books. Originally these writings were written on skin or parchment and made up into individual rolls or scrolls.

Of course, there are many ancient copies of the Hebrew Bible, and these are often referred to as "manuscripts". Until the discovery of the Dead Sea Scrolls in 1947, it was thought that the oldest manuscript dated from the ninth century. However, manuscripts discovered in caves beside the Dead Sea have been dated as far back as the second century B.C.

Because the common language in the days of the ancient Israelites was Hebrew, the Hebrew Bible (called the Old Testament by Christians) was written in that language except for a small portion in the books of Daniel and Ezra-Nehemiah which was in Aramaic (a Semitic dialect closely related to Hebrew). The contents of the Hebrew Bible are the same as those of the Old Testament in the Christian scriptures, but they are arranged differently. The Hebrew Bible is divided into three main parts:

> THE TEACHING (Torah), which consists of five books:
>   Genesis, Exodus, Leviticus, Numbers and Deuteronomy
> THE PROPHETS (Nebhi'im), which consists of eight books:
>   Former Prophets: Joshua, Judges, Samuel and Kings
>   Latter Prophets: Isaiah, Jeremiah, Ezekiel and the twelve minor prophets

A worshipper in a synagogue is wearing his prayer shawl (*talis*). Boxes containing portions of the Torah (*tefellin*) are strapped to his arm and forehead. The prayer shawl is decorated with fringes and is a reminder of God's commandments (see Numbers 15:37-41). The boxes are strapped to his arm (which is close to the heart) and forehead (which is close to the mind) as an indication of the dedication of heart and mind to God. Here, the worshipper is pointing to the sacred Torah scroll which is usually kept inside the Ark of the Covenant. (Courtesy of Ray Kurkjian)

THE WRITINGS (Kethubhim), which consists of eleven books:
    Poetry: Psalms, Proverbs and Job
    The Five Scrolls: Song of Solomon, Ruth, Lamentations,
    Ecclesiastes and Esther
    History: Ezra-Nehemiah and Chronicles
    Prophecy: Daniel

Of these, the most important is the Torah. Traditionally the authorship of the Torah is ascribed to Moses, but many modern biblical scholars think that, although Moses may have written the substance of the Ten Commandments and the Book of the Covenant (Exodus 24), the five books in the form in which we now have them were written and edited by later scribes. In any case, the importance of the Torah lies in the basic concepts and fundamental views that it conveys.

The Torah
The Hebrew word *Torah* is a term which has been traditionally translated as our word "Law". In modern times, however, it has been frequently pointed out that such a translation is misleading as well as

inaccurate, since the Torah contains more than legal prescriptions. Hence, the proposed modern rendering is "The Teaching" or "Instruction".

The Torah is an account of the history of the ancient Hebrew people, from the days of their exodus from Egypt, under the leadership of Moses, to the eve of their triumphant entry into the land of Canaan. Prefaced to this account is a history of the origin of the universe and mankind (Genesis 1-11), followed by the stories and sagas of the Patriarchs: Abraham, Isaac, Jacob and Joseph (Genesis 11-50). Scattered among the accounts about Moses and the narratives in the next four books (Exodus to Deuteronomy) are various codes of "law" or "instructions" delivered by God to Moses.

MOSES

The life of Moses is regarded as the cornerstone of Judaism. As the adopted son of an Egyptian princess, he was spared from the slavery which had been imposed upon his people, the Israelites. One day he witnessed a scene that became a turning point in his life: an Egyptian beating an Israelite. Moved by a sudden outburst of anger, Moses struck the Egyptian and killed him on the spot. As soon as he realized that rumours of the killing were circulating, he fled eastward and settled in Midian. There he married Zepporah, the daughter of a Midianite priest, and had two sons.

A second turning point occurred while Moses was herding his father-in-law's flock of sheep near the sacred mountain of Horeb. There he experienced the presence of a divine being that not only changed his life but altered the destiny of his people.

> And the angel of the Lord appeared to him in a flame of fire out of the midst of a bush; and he looked, and lo, the bush was burning, yet it was not consumed. And Moses said, "I will turn aside and see this great sight, why the bush is not burnt." When the Lord saw that he turned aside to see, God called to him out of the bush, "Moses, Moses!" And he said, "Here am I." Then He said, "Do not come near; put off your shoes from your feet, for the place on which you are standing is holy ground. . . . I have seen the affliction of my people who are in Egypt, and have heard their cry because of their taskmasters. . . . Come, I will send you to Pharaoh that you may bring forth my people, the sons of Israel, out of Egypt."
>
> Exodus 3:2-10

Reluctant to accept such a responsible mission, Moses answered, "If I go to the people of Israel and say to them, 'The God of your fathers has sent me to you,' and they ask me 'What is His name?' what shall I say to them?" The reply he received was, "I AM WHO I AM. . . . Say this to the people of Israel, I AM has sent me to you."

The escape of the enslaved Israelites from Egypt (celebrated annually by the Passover Feast) as well as their safe arrival at the foot of the sacred Mount Horeb – sometimes referred to as Mount Sinai – are proofs of the dynamic leadership of Moses. At Mount Sinai, with Moses acting as the intermediary, a confrontation between God and the people of Israel resulted in a solemn pact, commonly known as a "covenant".

> Now therefore, if you will obey my voice and keep my covenant, you shall be my own possession among all peoples; for all the earth is mine, and you shall be to me a kingdom of priests and a holy nation . . .
>
> Exodus 19:5-6

The Torah is read on Sabbath days, festivals, and on Monday and Thursday mornings in the synagogue. In the course of one year the entire Torah is read. Next to the scroll is the covering which fits over the upper end of the roller. (Courtesy of Ray Kurkjian)

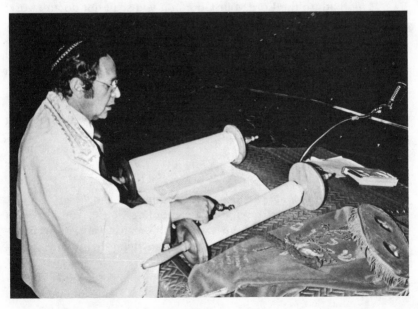

From the covenant came the Ten Commandments. Engraved on two stone tablets and delivered by God to Moses, they were to serve – and still serve – as the basis of the covenant. These stone tablets were put in an "Ark" and carried about by the Israelites in their journeys until they were finally placed in the temple built by Solomon in Jerusalem.

The Ten Commandments

1. I am the Lord your God, who brought you out of the land of Egypt, out of the house of bondage. *You shall have no other gods besides me.*
2. *You shall not make yourself a graven image,* or any likeness of anything that is in heaven above, or that is in the earth beneath, or that is in the water under the earth; you shall not bow to them or serve them; for I the Lord your God am a jealous God, visiting the iniquity of the fathers upon the children to the third and fourth generation of those who hate me, but showing steadfast love to thousands of those who love me and keep my commandments.
3. *You shall not take the name of the Lord your God in vain,* for the Lord will not hold him guiltless who takes his name in vain.
4. *Remember the sabbath day, to keep it holy.* Six days you shall labour, and do all your work; but the seventh day is a sabbath to the Lord your God; in it you shall not do any work, you, or your son, or your daughter, your manservant, or your maidservant, or your cattle, or the sojourner who is within your gates; for in six days the Lord made heaven and earth, the sea, and all that is in them, and rested the seventh day; therefore the Lord blessed the sabbath day and hallowed it.
5. *Honour your father and your mother,* that your days may be long in the land which the Lord your God gives you.
6. *You shall not kill.*
7. *You shall not commit adultery.*
8. *You shall not steal.*
9. *You shall not bear false witness against your neighbour.*
10. *You shall not covet* your neighbour's house; you shall not covet your neighbour's wife, or his manservant, or his maidservant, or his ox, or his ass, or anything that is your neighbour's.

Exodus 20:1-17
Deuteronomy 5:6-21

Among the Jews, Moses has always been and continues to be regarded as the chief of prophets. Again and again he insisted, as did all succeeding prophets, that, because of the covenant, Israel was a "special" people, a "chosen" race, as long as the people served God faithfully. This was not the result of Israel's merits, but a divine choice. Later prophets maintained that Israel was "chosen" not for her own glorification, but so that she might give light to other nations. If Israel failed in her mission then she had been unfaithful to the covenant.

The Prophets

THE FORMER PROPHETS

If the heart of Judaism is the Torah, then its mind is the literature known as The Prophets. The prophetic movement in ancient Israel began around the middle of the eleventh century B.C., although a few individuals before this time have been referred to as prophets. For instance, the Patriarch Abraham is considered a prophet (Genesis 20:7) in the sense of one who intercedes between God and man. Moses is designated a prophet (Deuteronomy 18:15; 34:10), though his place in Judaic tradition is more closely related to the role of leader – a man who speaks on behalf of God in a very special sense. There were also prophetesses, such as Miriam, Moses' sister (Exodus 15:20) and Deborah (Judges 4:4). But the earliest references to an established prophetic order appear during the time of Samuel and Saul in the middle of the eleventh century B.C.

Endowed with a vision sometimes called "second sight", the early prophets were thought of as "seers". The most famous of these was Samuel (I Samuel 9:5-9), although he was also considered a priest.

There also existed bands of ecstatic prophets who apparently moved about the country and played various musical instfuments (I Samuel 10:5-6). Whether or not such bands were regarded as guilds of prophets is now difficult to say; but some prophetic bands lived together in semi-monastic fashion, having their meals in common, in a community somewhat like a modern commune. The number of members in these communal prophetic orders varied from one hundred (I Kings 18:33) to as many as four hundred (I Kings 22:6). Moreover, each band must have been organized under a leader, like Elisha (II Kings 4:38; 6:1). Though they may have supported themselves to some extent, by and large they seem to have been dependent on the gifts of others (I Kings 14:3; II Kings 5:15; 8:9).

The kings of ancient Israel both consulted and retained at their royal courts many prophets who were qualified to interpret oracles and use divinatory methods to deliver important messages. For instance, King

Ahab and Jehosophat summoned four hundred prophets before attempting a military venture (I Kings 22).

The former prophets, who appeared between the eleventh and the eighth century B.C., are usually regarded as the "pre-literary" prophets. This simply means that their sayings or oracles were not recorded in writing; if they were recorded, then they have not come down to us. Furthermore, these prophets were men who were primarily interested in the immediate effects of their words and deeds rather than in lasting recognition of their authorship.

While many prophets were members of organized bands, some were totally independent thinkers who revolted against establishments and existing regimes. Such a prophet was Nathan, who had the courage to rebuke King David, first for having an affair with someone else's wife and later for arranging the murder of the husband when she became pregnant (II Samuel 12:1-15). Ahijah was another pronounced prophet and a "separatist" at heart. Not only was he connected with a revolution, but he instigated and supported the division of Israel's kingdom into two after Solomon's death (I Kings 11:26-40). Similarly, Elisha inspired the army commander Jehu to revolt against Ahab his king and claim the throne (II Kings 9).

Hence, the former prophets were of several varieties. Some were members of organized groups, while others were strong individualists. Some were experts in delivering oracles on important occasions, while others were bold enough to deliver moral judgement even on their own kings. Some were associated in one way or another with the royal courts, while others openly revolted against the ruling king. Many were ecstatic, while a few opposed ecstacy.

Not all prophets were highly regarded; many were objects of suspicion and contempt, as well as accused of being false prophets. Micaiah ben Imlah deserves to remembered as the first prophet who boldly challenged the unanimous prediction of the four hundred false prophets (I Kings 22). Their oracle to King Ahab was one that promised safety and victory if the king undertook the military campaign against Ramoth-Gilead. Micaiah's oracle foretold the king's death and defeat. Similarly, the dramatic contest of Elijah with the false prophets of Baal on Mount Carmel culminated in the killing of hundreds of them (I Kings 18:19-40). Nevertheless, the impact of the former prophets paved the way for the dynamic independence and moral concern of the latter prophets.

THE LATTER PROPHETS

It is unfortunate that prophets and Biblical prophecy are usually associated with the notion of prediction. While they did now and then anticipate success or failure, the main function of the latter prophets was to mold and shape the religious and moral pattern of ancient Israel. As a matter of fact, they were chiefly responsible for the progress, development and character of Judaism. Through a period of two centuries, (eighth to sixth century B.C.) they gradually replaced the idea of a tribal, jealous and national God with the idea of a God who was the God of the whole world. Moreover, they were deeply concerned with the social systems, institutions and practices of their time. Thus, as one Jewish author has expressed it, "They reformed Yahvism (from Yahveh, the name of the tribal god) from end to end, so that when they were done it was no longer Yahvism at all – it was Judaism!"

The first of these prophets was Amos, a herdsman, who suddenly appeared one day in the market place at Beth-El and in no uncertain terms pronounced first the judgement coming upon the surrounding nations and then the impending doom of Israel (Amos 1 and 2).

> Thus says the Lord: "For three transgressions of Israel, and for four, I will not revoke the punishment; because they sell the righteous for silver, and the needy for a pair of shoes – they that trample the head of the poor into the dust of the earth, and turn aside the way of the afflicted . . . "
>
> Amos 2:6-7

What is Amos opposing so daringly? Why, what else, if not what most great men everywhere and in all ages have strongly reacted against: social injustice. Men through the centuries have yearned for social justice. No amount of religious performance can ever justify the conscience of a society if cruelty, oppression and injustice are tolerated. Here once again are the words of Amos:

> Therefore thus says the Lord . . .
> "I hate, I despise your feasts, and I take no delight in your solemn assemblies.
> Even though you offer me your burnt offerings and cereal offerings,
> I will not accept them, and the peace offerings of your fatted beasts
> I will not look upon.
> Take away from me the noise of your songs; to the melody of your harps I will not listen.
> But let justice roll down like waters, and righteousness like an ever-flowing stream."
>
> Amos 5:21-24

Amos does not seem to be concerned about whether or not Israel is faithful to the covenant and the Torah. Nor does he condemn the people for idolatry. Rather, he strongly rebukes them for their unrighteous attitude and unjust activity. His God is a righteous God who expects his chosen people to reflect the divine image of justice and righteousness in their daily activities.

A younger contemporary of Amos was the prophet Hosea, a man of very different temperament. Like Amos, his message was a message of judgement, but surprisingly supplemented by his remarkable new insight about God. Israel seemed to Hosea much like his own unfaithful wife Gomer, who had deserted him in pursuit of "foreign" lovers. Just as Hosea later restored Gomer to his home, so God was to restore the wayward, unfaithful Israel. Hosea believed that, despite Israel's infidelity to the covenant, God loved Israel.

If Amos portrayed a righteous and just God, and Hosea portrayed a loving and merciful God, then it was left for Isaiah to capture another aspect of God – his holiness.

> Holy, holy, holy is the Lord of hosts; the whole earth is full of his glory.
>
> Isaiah 6:3

Isaiah was a courageous prophet who lived in Jerusalem. He was married, had at least two children and acted as an adviser in the royal court of Judah. Like Amos, he was more concerned about social behaviour than methods of worship. Hence he challenged and rebuked the hypocritical attitude of the people in his day (how like our modern times). There was no sense, he said, in performing any religious ceremonies or feasts or prayers when social injustice, oppression and cruelty was condoned and practised.

> "What to me is the multitude of your sacrifices?"
> says the Lord;
> "I have had enough of burnt offerings of rams and the fat of fed beasts;
> I do not delight in the blood of bulls,
> or of lambs, or of he-goats.
> When you come to appear before me,
> who requires of you this trampling of my courts?
> Bring no more vain offerings;
> incense is an abomination to me.
> New moon and sabbath and the calling of assemblies –
> I cannot endure iniquity and solemn assembly.

> Your new moons and your appointed feasts my soul hates;
> they have become a burden to me,
> I am weary of bearing them.
> When you spread forth your hands,
> I will hide my eyes from you;
> even though you make many prayers,
> I will not listen;
> your hands are full of blood.
> Wash yourselves; make yourselves clean;
> remove the evil of your doings from before my eyes;
> cease to do evil,
> learn to do good;
> seek justice,
> correct oppression;
> defend the fatherless,
> plead for the widow."
>
> Isaiah 1:11-17

Naturally Isaiah's stern words went unheeded; for while ancient Israel understood his oracles of doom pronounced over Babylon, Philistia, Moab, Damascus, Ethiopia, and Egypt, they could not comprehend the woes he foresaw for Israel. Haunted by the vision of divine holiness, Isaiah clearly envisioned God as the Lord not only of Israel but of all nations. Moreover, God's judgement would soon come like a flame to consume and purify; Isaiah did not have the slightest doubt that the armies of the invading empires would be the instruments of God to execute judgement over Israel.

Micah, following the tradition established by his predecessors, spoke out against religious formalism and ritualism. He too was less concerned about forms of worship than social behaviour. He stressed that ethical and moral obligations – principles related to human character and conduct of daily life – were more important than ceremonial religiosity:

> With what shall I come before the Lord,
> and bow myself before God on high?
> Shall I come before him with burnt offerings,
> with calves a year old?
> Will the Lord be pleased with thousands of rams,
> with ten thousands of rivers of oil?
> Shall I give my first-born for my transgression,
> the fruit of my body for the sin of my soul?

> He has showed you, O man, what is good;
> and what does the Lord require of you:
> but to do justice,
> and to love kindness,
> and to walk humbly with your God!
>
> Micah 6:8

While Isaiah altered the narrow, nationalistic concept of God, traditional of Judaism, it was Jeremiah who finally shattered it. It was the prophet Jeremiah who ran counter to the dominant public sentiment of the day. Naturally, he was opposed and persecuted; nevertheless he insisted that God was supremely an ethical God and the Lord of the whole world. Hence, nothing short of a "change of heart" would be acceptable to God. He furthermore stressed the "inwardness" of religion; he defined true piety as the personal relationship of an individual to God. He envisioned God as wanting to write a "new covenant", not, as previously, on tablets of stone delivered to Moses, but on the hearts of individuals.

> "Behold the days are coming," says the Lord, "when I will make a new covenant . . . not like the covenant which I made with their fathers . . . which they broke . . . But this is the covenant which I will make . . . I will put my law within them, and I will write it upon their hearts; and I will be their God, and they shall be my people."
>
> Jeremiah 31:31-34

Obviously it is impossible to discuss all the latter prophets in this brief survey; but a few of the outstanding ones have been mentioned. Consciously or unconsciously, these prophets gradually shaped and molded the character of Judaism, and their writings later exerted a tremendous influence on Christianity.

The Writings
Although the Torah represents the most powerful influence in Judaism and the Prophets shaped its ethical and moral character, its inspirational genius lies in the Writings. The Writings consists of a varied collection of poetic, proverbial and philosophic material. In fact, one of the most interesting and important elements in the development of Judaism is the work of the unknown sages whose wisdom has come down to us in the Writings. It includes, for example, the book of Proverbs, a collection of wise maxims and epigrams; the book of Psalms, at once the hymnal and prayer book of Judaism, to say nothing

of its incalculable impact upon Christianity; the book of Job, which dramatizes the philosophical problem of good and evil and why the good suffer; and the universal quest for the purpose of existence, profoundly expressed in the book of Qoheleth (Ecclesiastes).

The striking feature of the Writings is the shift in outlook. The interest of these sages was not particularly in Judaism, nor in national interests, but in humanity. They addressed their listeners as men and struggled with universal human problems. Hence, they might be called "humanists". Their sayings deal with the whole range of life: personal affairs, family relations, social and business matters, public interests, manners, and morals. We will now look at some of their work.

PROVERBS

There is a wealth of wisdom and observation, of humour and sarcasm, of exhortation and appeal, in the book of Proverbs. Here is a poem dedicated to alcoholics.

To Alcoholics

Who has woe? Who has sorrow?
Who has strife? Who has complaining?
Who has wounds without cause?
Who has redness of eyes?

Those who tarry long over wine,
Those who go to try mixed wine.

Do not look at wine when it is red,
When it sparkles in the cup and goes down smoothly.
At the last it bites like a serpent,
And stings like an adder.

Your eyes will see strange things,
And your mind will utter perverse things.

You will be like one who lies down in the midst of the sea,
Like one who lies on the top of a mast.
"They struck me," you will say, "but I was not hurt;
They beat me, but I did not feel it."

"When shall I awake?
I will seek another drink."

Proverbs 23:29-35

The sages teach that a happy and prosperous life belongs to those who attain knowledge and wisdom.

> A wise man is mightier than a strong man,
> and a man of knowledge than he who has strength.
>
> Proverbs 24:5

But the wise man is described as one who follows moral and religious principles in order that he may be happy. The tone of the sages is similar to the latter prophets. They express prophetic thought in the form of maxims:

> To do righteousness and justice
> is more acceptable to the Lord than sacrifice.
>
> Proverbs 21:3

> He who oppresses a poor man insults his Maker,
> but he who is kind to the needy honours him.
>
> Proverbs 14:31

> If a man returns evil for good,
> evil will not depart from his house.
>
> Proverbs 17:13

> If your enemy is hungry, give him bread to eat;
> and if he is thirsty, give him water to drink;
> for you will heap coals of fire on his head,
> and the Lord will reward you.
>
> Proverbs 25:21-22

The sages found the secret source of meaningful living in Wisdom – the supreme principle in man. Wisdom existed prior to creation and at creation "she" was the pervading principle functioning as a "master workman" (Proverbs 8:22-31). True living, then, consists in being in harmony with this universal principle (Wisdom), which reveals itself to the minds of men.

> Happy is the man who listens to me [Wisdom] . . .
> for he who finds me finds life
> and obtains favour from the Lord;
> but he who misses me injures himself;
> all who hate me love death.
>
> Proverbs 8:34-35

PSALMS

Another book that voices the needs of all generations is the book of Psalms. The whole range of human life is treated here, whether at the national level or at the level of the individual, with all life's joys and woes, its hopes and its fears. Here are hymns of trust, praise, and thanksgiving; but here also are passionate pleas for revenge over individual or national enemies. Here, too, are raised prayers for common worship, for individual help and healing, and for national restoration.

The book of Psalms repays reading and study for its own sake; a few examples of these ageless poems, revealing the deepest human feelings and desires, may suggest why this is so.

> Out of the depths I cry to thee, O Lord!
> Lord, hear my voice!
> Let thy ears be attentive to the voice of my supplications!
>
> Psalms 130:1-2

> Bless the Lord, O my soul;
> and all that is within me, bless his holy name!
> Bless the Lord, O my soul;
> and forget not all his benefits . . .
>
> Psalms 103:1-2

> O sing to the Lord a new song;
> sing to the Lord all the earth!
> Sing to the Lord, bless his name;
> tell of his salvation from day to day.
> Declare his glory among the nations,
> his marvelous works among all the peoples!
>
> Psalms 96:1-3

> Even though I walk through the valley of the shadow of death,
> I fear no evil;
> for Thou art with me;
> Thy rod and Thy staff, they comfort me.
>
> Psalms 23:4

JOB

Two immortal classics are the books of Job and Qoheleth (Ecclesiastes). Each views life from a different viewpoint.

One of the traditional views (and a view still held by many) was that the righteous would be prosperous and favoured by God while the wicked would be overtaken by calamity; or, to put it differently, that the cause of suffering was one's own sin or wickedness. The book of Job challenges the validity of this concept; it shows that the facts of life contradict this theory: the wicked may prosper and lead a happy life, while the righteous may suffer and be overtaken by tragedy.

From the outset, it is made clear that Job is blameless and righteous (Job 1:1). But can Job maintain his integrity unless his devotion is rewarded by prosperity? If he loses everything he possesses, including wealth, children, and his own health, will he still trust God? The story clearly indicates how Job stands the test. All the time that he suffers, his three friends doubt his righteousness; but Job knows that he is innocent. His friends try to explain Job's suffering by examining Job. Job seeks the reason for his suffering by examining God! His friends declare that Job is a sinner; Job declares that God is unjust! (Job 16:18-21; 31:1-40.)

The story concludes without explaining the cause of Job's suffering. Nevertheless, the point clearly made is that true piety needs no outward proof of success, for God is righteous and rules the world righteously, no matter how incomprehensible his rule may seem to be.

QOHELETH

From the earliest times to the present, the book of Ecclesiastes (in Hebrew called Qoheleth) has attracted the attention of many thinkers. "Vanity of vanities, everything is vanity!": this is its initial note and its conclusion (Ecclesiastes 1:2; 12:28). The remainder of the work illustrates, with a series of wide-ranging examples drawn from the world of nature and the world of man, in what sense everything is "vanity".

The Hebrew term *habhel* literally means "breath" or "vapour", and figuratively, therefore, implies impermanence, transitoriness. Hence, the English rendering of "vanity" for *habhel* should not be understood in its modern sense as "the subjective attitude of false pride", but should be considered figuratively as meaning the worthlessness or impermanence of all that happens.

The sweeping statement of Qoheleth that everything in life is impermanent, that like a "vapour" or "breath" it is visible only for a short time, (Ecclesiastes 1:2, 14; 2:17; 3:19), is the result of investigation in at least five major areas in life:

TOIL. Life is such that man must of necessity work; but the mere possibility that the fruit of one's skill and labour may work to the advantage or fall into the possession of someone who may never have to strive for it, proves the vanity of toil (Ecclesiastes 2:4-21). Furthermore, Qoheleth observes two base motives underlying the impulse of active labour: the jealousy that drives a man to compete with his neighbour (Ecclesiastes 4:4) and the greed that impels him to accumulate possessions even though he may not have a single surviving heir to whom he can leave them (Ecclesiastes 4:7-8). What is the reward of such toil? Days filled with sorrow and pain, and nights filled with restlessness. Hence Qoheleth regards toil as a vanity.

PLEASURE. If what is "good" in life is to be found anywhere, surely it must be in gaiety. Qoheleth therefore explores the pleasurable aspects of human activity. But the conclusion drawn from "having a good time" is that pleasure and laughter are also vanity.

WISDOM. Disillusioned both with toil and pleasure, Qoheleth probes the value of wisdom. Wisdom, it is quickly established, is better than ignorance (Ecclesiastes 2:13). But does not man's final fate – death – confront the fool as well as the wise man? The fact that the wise are swallowed by the same oblivion as the foolish (Ecclesiastes 2:14-16) makes Qoheleth pronounce the pursuit of wisdom to be vanity, too (Ecclesiastes 1:16).

WEALTH. Utterly disappointed with toil and pleasure, and bitterly dissatisfied with wisdom, the author of Qoheleth now turns to investigate the value of wealth. His keen insight leads him first to observe that contrary to what many may believe, wealth has nothing to do with ability or merit (Ecclesiastes 9:11). Wealth is not an outcome of intelligence, but purely of time and chance. Moreover, since no one may take his riches with him at death, the pursuit of wealth is vanity.

MORALS. Qoheleth's observations lead him to the conclusion that Providence is unconcerned with moral distinctions. The wicked and the righteous are treated alike (Ecclesiastes 9:2). As a matter of fact, the wicked prosper and are rewarded with power, while the righteous are oppressed and go unheeded. To follow piety is indeed "vain" since good and evil are so divinely mixed. Moreover, since the destiny of human beings is similar to the destiny of beasts, why should men bother to live a righteous life? If death robs life of meaning and purpose, then life itself, Qoheleth concludes, is transitory and purposeless – in other words, "vanity of vanities!"

The conclusion that Qoheleth reaches after a long process of investigation is not one of pessimism or resignation. Since the riddle of life is bounded by the riddle of death – the common fate of all – then life is transitory, says Qoheleth. This does not mean that life has no purpose or is meaningless as some modern thinkers and philosophers have asserted. Far from making such a statement, Qoheleth asserts that life is a riddle, a mystery; that no one will ever understand it. The writer does not deny the existence of God, but simply affirms that God's purpose is incapable of being discovered by inquiry. In other words, life is inscrutable, and the only conclusion that can be stated with any confidence is that life is transitory.

Traditions: Talmud and Midrash

By the time the Hebrew Bible had been completed and assembled, great changes had taken place within Judaism. These changes gave rise to oral interpretation and traditions concerning many of the written laws. Though Judaism has firmly held to the binding character of the Torah, it has equally respected the Traditions. The Talmud, which

Studying the Torah with its Talmudic commentaries is the duty of every devout Jew. Like prayer, study is a way of worshipping God; hence the head is covered. The covering of the head is an indication of respect for and awareness of God's presence. (Courtesy of Ray Kurkjian)

consisted at first mainly of oral traditions, grew out of the conviction that besides the written Torah there should be also a collection of "oral Torah". Being a collection of commentaries, of traditions and precedents, the Talmud supplements the Scriptures as a source of authority.

After several centuries, these oral traditions were gradually recorded and organized as a collection of Oral Law consisting of six "orders" (volumes) sub-divided by topics into sixty-three "tractates" (divisions). This collection of Oral Law (recorded like the Torah in Hebrew) was called the Mishnah. Later, however, Jews spoke and taught in Aramaic instead of Hebrew. The change from one language to another necessitated commentaries and explanations of the Mishnah. The result was a collection of commentaries known as the Gemarah. The Mishnah, together with the Gemarah, which run to some forty volumes, are jointly know as the Talmud.

As a product of two distinct Judaic centres of learning, two Talmudic versions exist: the Palestinian and the Babylonian. One explanation which accounts for the differences between the two versions in subject matter, method, presentation and language is the life style of the Jews who lived in Palestine as opposed to the Jews who lived in Babylonia. Biblical commandments had to be applied differently in different circumstances. Today decisions in matters of religious law are rendered on the basis of the Babylonian Talmud. Here are some excerpts:

> Rabbi Joshua said, "Wherever you find a description of the greatness of the Holy One, praised be He, you find a description of His consideration for the lowly. This is written in the Torah, repeated in the Prophets, and stated for the third time in the Writings. In the Torah it is written: 'For the Lord your God is God of gods and Lord of lords . . . ' (Deuteronomy 10:17) and in the verse following it is written, 'He executes justice for the fatherless and the widow' (Deuteronomy 10:18). It is repeated in the Prophets: 'For thus says the high and lofty One who inhabits eternity, whose name is holy: I dwell in the high and holy place' (Isaiah 57:15). And the verse continues 'and also with him who is of a contrite and humble spirit'. It is stated for the third time in the Writings: 'Extol Him who rides upon the skies, whose name is the Lord,' (Psalms 68:5) and in the verse following it is written, 'Father of the fatherless and protector of widows' " (Psalms 68:6).

> Megillah 31a

"Then Moses said to God 'If I come to the people of Israel and say to them "The God of your fathers has sent me to you" and they ask "What is His name?" what shall I say to them?' " (Exodus 3:13). Moses asked the Holy One, praised be He, to tell him His great name. "And God said to Moses 'I am what I am' " (Exodus 3:14). Rabbi Abba bar Mamal said: The Holy One, praised be He, said to Moses "You want to know My name. I am called according to My deeds. At various times I am called Almighty Lord of hosts, God, and Lord. When I judge My creatures, I am called God. When I wage war against the wicked, I am called Lord of hosts. When I suspend the punishment of man's sins, I am called Almighty. And when I have compassion upon My world, I am called Lord. Thus Scripture states 'I am what I am; I am called according to My deeds.' "

Exodus Rabbah 3:6

After Moses, David came and reduced the six hundred and thirteen commandments to eleven, as it is written: "Lord, who shall sojourn in Your tabernacle? Who shall dwell on Your holy mountain. He who walks blamelessly, and does what is right, and speaks truth in his heart, who does not slander with his tongue, and does no evil to his friend, nor takes up a reproach against his neighbour, in whose eyes a reprobate is despised, but honours those who fear the Lord, who swears to his own hurt and does not change, who does not put out his money at interest, and does not take a bribe against the innocent" (Psalms 15:1-5).

Then Isaiah came and reduced the commandments to six, as it is written, "He who walks righteously and speaks uprightly, he who despises the gain of oppressions, who shakes his hands lest they hold a bribe, who stops his ears from hearing of bloodshed, and shuts his eyes from looking upon evil" (Isaiah 33:15) . . . Then Micah came and reduced them to three, as it is written, "It has been told you, O man what is good, and what the Lord requires of you: To do justice, to love mercy, and to walk humbly with your God" (Micah 6:8) . . . Then Isaiah came again and reduced them to two. "Thus says the Lord: Keep justice and do righteousness" (Isaiah 56:1). Amos came and reduced them to one, as it is written, "Thus says the Lord to the house of Israel: Seek Me and live" (Amos

5:4) . . . Habakkuk came and also reduced them to one, as it is written, "The righteous shall live by his faith" (Habakkuk 2:4).

Makkot 24a

Rabbi Huna and Rabbi Jeremiah said in the name of the Rabbi Hiyya-bar Aba: It is written, "They have forsaken Me and have not kept My law" (Jeremiah 16:11). This is to say: "If only they had forsaken Me but kept My law! Since they then would have been occupied with it, the light which is in it would have restored them to the right path."

Lamentations Rabbah II

Resh Lakish said: "The commandment of the Lord is pure" (Psalms 19:9). If one's intent is pure, the Torah for him becomes a life-giving medicine, purifying him to life. But if one's intent is not pure, it becomes a death-giving drug, purifying him to death.

Yoma 72b

This was a favourite saying of the rabbis of Javneh: I am a creature of God and my neighbour is also His creature; my work is in the city and his in the field; I rise early to my work and he rises early to his. As he cannot excel in my work, so I cannot excel in his. You might say that I do great things while he does small things. However we have learned that it matters not whether a man does much or little, if only he directs his heart toward Heaven.

Berakhot 17a

Rabbi Eliezer said: the nations (i.e., non-Jews) will have no share in the world to come, as it is written "The wicked shall depart to Sheol, and all the nations that forget God" (Psalms 9:17). The first part of the verse refers to the wicked among Israel. However, Rabbi Joshua said to him: If the verse had stated "The wicked shall depart to Sheol, and all the nations," I would agree with you. But the verse goes on to say "that forget God". Therefore it means to say that there are righteous men among the other nations of the world who do have a share in the world to come.

Tosefta Sanhedrin 13:2

Midrash is the name given to the collection of literary works which contain Scriptural expositions and interpretations of either legal (Halakah) or non-legal (Haggadah) character. The term *Midrash* stems from a Hebrew word which means "to search out, to investigate": hence, "to expound".

Next to the Hebrew Bible, the most sacred Jewish books are the Talmud and the Midrash, which usually require a lifetime of study. The three excerpts which follow illustrate how the Talmud also mirrors or echoes the basic ethics of Judaism:

> Love him who reproves you, that you may add wisdom to your wisdom; hate him who praises you, that your wisdom may not diminish.
> Judge not your neighbour till you are in his place.
> Without religion there can be no true morality; without morality there can be no true religion.

Religious Concepts

GOD

The God of Judaism is One and there is no other god beside him. "In the beginning God created the heavens and the earth" are the opening words of the Torah. Starting with the assumption that *God is*, the writings in the Torah never regard God's existence as something to be proved. The very essence of Judaism is firmly stated in one sentence: "Hear, O Israel: the Lord our God, the Lord is One!" It is the first prayer that a Jew learns as a child and it is the last prayer upon his lips before he dies.

There is a story that an emperor who wanted to prove God's existence once asked a prominent Rabbi to show him God.

"But you cannot see him," replied the Rabbi.

"Nevertheless, I want to see him," insisted the emperor. Leading him out to the open courtyard, the Rabbi asked the emperor to look straight up at the sun.

"But I cannot," replied the emperor.

"If you cannot look at the sun," retorted the Rabbi, "which is but one of the servants who stand in the presence of the Holy One, praised be He, then how can you see God?"

The Torah represents God as a personal God; not in the sense that he has a physical body, but in that he enters, instructs and directs the life of man. Moreover, he is regarded as "merciful and gracious, slow to anger, and abounding in steadfast love and fruitfulness" (Exodus 34:6-7). He is "God of gods and Lord of lords, the great, the mighty, and the terrible God (Deuteronomy 10:17) who executes justice for the orphan and the widow. Nevertheless, He is a "jealous God, visiting the iniquity of the fathers upon the children to the third and fourth generation of those who hate Him, but showing steadfast love to thousands who love Him and keep His commandments" (Exodus 20:5).

In other words, those who love God and keep his commandments benefit from the love, mercy, and grace of God, whereas those who disobey his commandment only reap his anger and justice. There is no paradox, no apparent problem between God's mercy and his justice. A later Rabbinic commentary explains it this way: if the world had been created on the basis of God's mercy alone, then the sins of the world would have been many; if on the other hand the world had been created strictly on the basis of God's justice, then the world would not have been able to exist; hence, to maintain a proper balance, God created the world with both his attributes – justice and mercy.

On all doorposts (in homes, offices, schools) the *mezuzzah* symbolizes God's presence. This custom is based on the biblical passage of Deuteronomy 6:4-9. (Courtesy of Ray Kurkjian)

Of course, in the time of the Israelites people worshipped other "gods"; they practised idolatry and assumed polytheistic customs and rites (Deuteronomy 32:17). Nevertheless, God raised up courageous men, known as "prophets", who were unconcerned with their own lives so long as they could clearly protest and remind the people of their "covenant" with the living God. Some were stoned, others were imprisoned, and others still were destined to be exiled; yet, through their powerful message, the prophets left their indelible mark:

> Thus says the Lord, the King of Israel and his redeemer, the Lord of hosts: "I am the first and I am the last; besides me there is no god. Who is like me? Let him proclaim it, let him declare and set it forth before me . . . Is there a god besides me? . . . "

> All who make idols are nothing, and the things they delight in do not profit; their witnesses neither see nor know, that they may be put to shame.
>
> Isaiah 44:6-9

Again and again, these prophets echoed the same message: Hear, O Israel, the Lord our God, the Lord is One! In spite of numerous warnings, the Israelites persisted in their polytheistic attitudes and in magical and divinatory practices until both kingdoms were finally conquered by foreign invasion. (See II Kings 17:8-17, and 21:3-9.)

THE UNIVERSE

The Torah never suggests that the universe is self-created.

> In the beginning God created the heavens and the earth. The earth was without form and void, and darkness was upon the face of the deep . . .
>
> Genesis 1:1-2

God is regarded as the creator of the heavens and earth. Everything that is has come into being by his command, and nothing exists without his will. " 'Let there be,' said He, and there was." God's commanding word separated darkness from light, night from day, the heavens from the earth. The sun, moon and all the heavenly bodies came into being at his word. He separated the seas from the dry land and then ordered the waters to bring forth all sorts of creatures, while the earth was to produce vegetation, plants, fruits, as well as bring forth all kinds of living creatures and animals. For his last act of creation God fashioned man "in His own image" and gave him the privilege of dominating and subduing the earth.

> And God said, "Be fruitful and multiply, and fill the earth and subdue it; and have dominion over . . . every living thing that moves upon the earth."
>
> Genesis 1:28

So firmly did the Hebrews believe that their God was not a spirit in nature, nor part of nature, but above and distinctively apart from nature, that they composed a hymn:

> O Lord, our Lord, how majestic is thy name in all
> the earth . . .
> When I look at thy heavens, the work of thy fingers,
> the moon and the stars which thou hast established;
> what is man that thou art mindful of him,
> and the son of man that thou dost care for him?
> Yet thou hast made him little less than God,
> and dost crown him with glory and honour.
> Thou hast given him dominion over the works of thy
> hands;
> Thou hast put all things under his feet,
> all sheep and oxen,
> and also the beasts of the field,
> the birds of the air, and the fish of the sea,
> whatever passes along the paths of the sea.
> O Lord, our Lord,
> how majestic is thy name in all the earth!
>
> Psalm 8

Neither the stars, nor the moon, nor any other heavenly or earthly phenomenon can be worshipped or thought to have god-like or divine characteristics. God alone brought everything into existence. He is the sole creator, preserver and ruler of the universe. This created universe is "good"; it was created according to God's will and for man's use. No one but God ordained the order of the universe.

MAN

Another viewpoint central to the Torah is that man is created in the image of God (Genesis 1:26; 5:21). Man must always be aware of this and realize that he is especially dear to God.

There is a story that once the Jewish scholar Hillel was asked where he was going. "I am going to perform a religious act (*mitzvah*)," he replied. When he was questioned further about this *mitzvah*, Hillel replied, "I am going to the bath house." Taken by surprise, Hillel's inquirer wanted to know how Hillel could interpret a bath as a religious act. "Those who are in charge of the images of Kings that are erected in public buildings rub and wash them and are honoured for it. How much more should I take care of my body, for I have been created in the image of God."

To be created in the image of God means, in the Jewish view, to be divinely ordained to demonstrate God's two attributes: justice and mercy. In other words, because God is just and merciful, man, who is created in the image of God, must also practise these two virtues. That there are temptations to evil in the world, and that man can descend to great depths of wickedness, Judaism will not deny. But Judaism believes that man's nature is not irretrievably sinful; his possibilities and potentialities are greater than his weaknesses.

Man's proper response to life is piety and reverence to God, and love and respect to his fellow-man. Judaism has never approved the renunciation of the world as a path of piety. Nowhere in the Torah is man instructed to detach himself from the world in order to please God. On the contrary, the pious man is the man who, like Hillel, loves the world and hallows life in such a way that his daily activities of eating, drinking, labouring and pleasure are raised to their highest level, so that all his acts are sacred and reflect the divine image.

Judaism prescribes in great detail how one ought to live in this world, since this world is regarded as God's gift to mankind. Moreover, it teaches that man's behaviour must be governed from the cradle to the grave by moral codes. Though God foresees and knows everything, man is free to choose and he is morally responsible for the choices he makes. He cannot, or rather, should not, blame God for his own misdeeds. There are no attempts in the Torah to offer philosophical explanations for these views; only the assertion that there is a God who judges man and that man is morally responsible for all his deeds.

> Behold, I set before you this day a blessing and a curse: the blessing, if you obey the commandments of the Lord your God . . . and the curse, if you do not obey the commandments of the Lord your God . . .
>
> Deuteronomy 11:26-28

While an ethical atmosphere seems to permeate Judaism, it must be acknowledged that it advocates three very basic qualities for the good life: good deeds, enjoyment of living, and love of fellow-man. There is little evidence in Judaism of asceticism (the rejection of bodily comforts), although it is a marked feature of other religions. Since the world is not considered inherently evil, there is no need to abandon it.

A very well known story relates how a heathen once came to the Jewish scholar Shammai and said that he would become a proselyte (convert to Judaism) on condition that he was taught the entire Torah while standing on one foot. Shammai chased him away, so the man appealed next to Hillel, another Jewish scholar. "Whatever is hateful to you," said Hillel to the man, "do not do to your neighbour; that is the entire Torah. The rest is commentary, go and learn it." By commentary Hillel meant the body of literature that resulted from a definition of love to one's fellow-man, the significance of enjoyment of living, and what constitutes good deeds.

Thus the central themes that dominate the Torah are interrelated themes: God, the universe and man. God is absolutely without rivals or incarnations and needs no representation. The universe is good and the purpose of man's life is to joyfully serve God and his fellow-man.

Practices and Institutions

One of the most ancient Jewish rituals, unchanged to the present day, is the ritual of circumcision. Ordained by God, this religious duty was first assigned to the Patriarch Abraham as a token of the fulfilment of an agreement or covenant.

> This is my covenant, which you shall keep . . . every male among you shall be circumcised . . . he that is eight days old among you shall be circumcised . . .
>
> Genesis 17:10-12

A second Jewish ritual is the Kashruth (Dietary Laws). Contemporary Reform Judaism rejects these laws even though many attempts have been made through the ages to explain and justify them. The Kashruth still remains the traditional Judaic way to holiness as a part of a total system. Many passages in the Torah make specific reference to regulations about permitted and forbidden foods. (See Leviticus 11:1-46; 17:10-14; Deuteronomy 14:21.)

Another tradition is the sanctity of one day during the week. Because God rested from his work of creation on the seventh day, Judaism reserves the Sabbath (Saturday) as a holy day. It is a day of "rest", and no work is done. Since the day is defined as the period between one sunset and the next, the Sabbath begins at dusk on Friday, when the

The Sabbath begins every Friday at sunset when members of the family gather around the table. First, the mother says a blessing over the candles and lights them. Next, the father takes a cup of wine and says a blessing over it, after which everyone takes a sip. Then the Sabbath loaf *(chalah)* is sliced by the father and shared by all. (Courtesy of George Morrison)

mother of the house says a blessing over lighted candles. Then the father takes a cup of wine and says a blessing over it before everyone takes a sip. Next the Sabbath loaf is sliced and shared, after which an evening meal may follow.

Of course, the Sabbath is not the only holy day; there are many other ceremonial days observed during the year which recall great events in the history of Judaism. To commemorate the "exodus" from Egypt under the leadership of Moses, Jews celebrate the feast of Pesach (the Passover). The supper celebrated in connection with the Passover feast resembles the Lord's Supper observed by Christians.

Fifty days after the Passover feast comes the Festival of the Weeks, known as Shabuoth or Pentecost. An ancient agricultural festival, which was marked by gathering the first fruits of the spring wheat harvest, Shabuoth is now commemorated as the day of encounter between God, Moses, and the people at Sinai.

Another ancient agricultural festival which marked the end of the harvest and is celebrated now much as Christians in North America celebrate Thanksgiving Day is the Feast of Tabernacles or the Sukkoth.

According to variations in the Jewish calendar, the Jewish New Year, known as Rosh Hashanah, falls around September or October. Ten days after Rosh Hashanah comes the Day of Atonement or Yom Kippur. These are the two most solemn days of the year and are devoted to soul-searching, confession of sins, repentance and reconciliation.

Naturally there are many other ceremonies celebrated in Judaism; Hannukah and Purim are two examples. The Festival of Hannukah (also called the Festival of Lights) is celebrated annually at about the same time that Christians celebrate Christmas. The term *hannukah* means "consecration" or "dedication", and this festival commemorates the cleansing of the Temple in 165 B.C. which marked the beginning of a period of religious liberty (led by the Hasmonean party). Purim is also an annual festival, celebrated during February-March in remembrance of the occasion when Esther and Mordecai frustrated Haman's scheme to destroy the Jews in the Persian empire. Characteristic of all such religious celebrations is the deep sense of God and the age-old covenant He made with Israel.

Just as Judaism is distinguished by characteristic ceremonies and festivals, so it is represented, like most other religions, by various distinct groups. In the pre-Christian period these were the Pharisees, the Sadducees, the Essenes and the Zealots.

Hannukah — the Festival of Lights — is celebrated annually in December. It is observed for eight days beginning on the twenty-fifth day of the month of Kislev. (Courtesy of Ray Kurkjian)

The Pharisees were chiefly concerned with religious instruction and conducting synagogue services outside the Temple in Jerusalem. They were the representatives of the religious beliefs, practices and social outlook of the masses. The Sadducees, on the other hand, were composed largely of the wealthy elements of the population: the prosperous merchants, the aristocrats, and the powerful priests. Although there were a great many legal and ritualistic details about which the Pharisees and Sadducees differed, two of their major differences lay in their attitudes towards the Oral Traditions and resurrection. The Sadducees refused to accept any of the Oral Traditions, whereas the Pharisees used them to supplement the Torah. The Sadducees denied any belief in the resurrection of the body whereas the Pharisees accepted it.

The Essenes were a small, devout, communal group who lived in the vicinity of Qumram by the Dead Sea. Our knowledge of the Essene

The Wadi Qumran area, where it is thought that the Essene community lived in caves and carried on its communal activities. The Dead Sea Scrolls and various biblical texts were discovered in eleven such caves. (Courtesy of B. Painter)

community, though scanty, has been greatly supplemented by the discovery in 1947 of the Dead Sea Scrolls. The discipline of the Essene community was very strict and they seem to have practised communal ownership of property.

The Zealots were fanatic patriots who refused any compromise with Rome and opposed the attempt to make Judea subservient to Roman powers. Against the advice of the Pharisees and the Sadducees, they rose in revolt against the Roman powers in A.D. 66. The Romans slowly, but methodically, crushed this revolt. In A.D. 70 Jerusalem fell, the Temple was burnt, and thousands of Jews were carried away as slaves to Rome. Another uprising however occurred from A.D. 132 to 135. The Romans once again reacted with calculated ruthlessness. The site of the Temple was totally devastated and thousands of Jews were scattered in a movement known as "the Dispersion". With no national home till the twentieth century the Jews looked to their leaders, the Rabbis (teachers), for religious guidance, the calendar of festivals, and teachings of laws and customs.

During the Middle Ages three new groups evolved: the Karaites, the Kabbalists and the Hassidics. The Karaites flourished in the Near East, especially in Babylonia (modern Iraq) from the ninth to the twelfth centuries. The name *Karaite* literally means "readers of scriptures". They were so called because of their exclusive adherence to the Bible as the only source of religious authority in Judaism. They repudiated the Talmud as a spurious invention of the Rabbis.

Although the Kabbalistic movement may have originated in Palestine, its systematic development took place in Babylonia. The term *kabel* means "to receive" and the name Kabbalist at first described any Jewish mystic who was a teacher of secret or inward revelation. Hence Kabbalist became the name associated with those Jews who were particularly concerned with the philosophical mystic lore of Judaism based upon an occult interpretation of the Bible handed down as secret doctrine to the initiated. During the ninth and tenth centuries the Kabbalistic movement spread to Europe, especially to Italy, Spain and Germany.

The two most important books of the movement composed and edited in Babylonia were the Sefer Yitzirah (The Book of Formation) and the Shiur Komah (The Measure of the Height). The former chiefly concerned the creative powers of letters and numbers, while the latter described in human terms the dimensions of the Deity. However the book which came to be regarded as the most sacred of all Kabbalistic writings, and the very epitome of Jewish mysticism, is the Zohar.

The word *zohar* means "splendour" or "brightness" and is derived from Daniel 12:3. The book records the revelations said to have been received in the second century A.D. by Rabbi Simeon ben Yochai, during the thirteen years he was hiding in a cave, and transmitted by him to his disciples. Compiled and made public in A.D. 1300 by Moses de Leon of Granada, Spain, the Zohar came to be regarded as the Bible of Medieval mysticism. The Zohar is a compendium of Jewish mystic lore on the nature of God, the mysteries of the Divine name, God's attributes and dimensions, the evolution of the universe, man's place in the universe and the nature of the human soul, the characteristics of heaven and hell, the order of the angels and demons, magic, astrology, as well as expositions on many ethical themes and ceremonies.

The Hassidics (the term *Hassid* means "pious") are a mystical group still represented in modern Judaism; their origins go back to the Kabbalist Israel Baal Shem Tob (A.D. 1700-1760). Famed as a miracle worker and healer, he was regarded as a true saint and a mystic. By the efforts of a number of his disciples, the movement attracted a large following, especially among the Jews of the Polish Ukraine. Despite opposition, Hassidism made great progress, and it is believed that during the first half of the nineteenth century the movement won over nearly half of all Jews. In contrast to Kabbalistic mysticism, which was difficult to understand and appealed particularly to intellectuals, Hassidic mysticism became a vital, singing faith of the masses. Its appeal lay less in visions of speedy Messianic deliverance, than in relieving day by day the gloom and depression of an impoverished people. Without suppressing the natural impulses of man, Hassidic mysticism promoted contentment coupled with meekness and modesty.

Modern Judaism is basically divided into three fairly well defined forms. Orthodox Judaism attempts to adhere rigidly to the practical admonitions of the Laws of Moses, as they are interpreted and applied to daily life by the Talmud. They regard the Torah not simply as a divine revelation, but final and complete, only awaiting fulfillment. It is perhaps fair, however, to say that the Orthodox Jews lay less emphasis on belief than on practice. The Orthodox Jew need not necessarily accept the rabbinical view but he must follow with absolute fidelity the Talmudic teachings on kashruth rules, Sabbath observance, and festivals, as well as avoid too much contact with the "outside" world.

At the other end of the spectrum is Reform Judaism, which has abandoned many traditional practices and has conformed to the "spirit" of the modern age. In North American society this has led to the simplification and modernization of Synagogue worship, an emphasis on ethical living, and an attempt to adapt to the ways of modern society.

Between the two extremes is Conservative Judaism, which, though it has forsaken a number of ancient practices, still retains some of the major rituals. Moreover, it reinterprets the Torah for modern times, although it cautiously avoids any tendency towards assimilation, to which it feels Reform Judaism is prone.

No matter what trends the future may bring, Judaism continues to be one of the religions which asserts that God exists and that He speaks today just as He spoke in the past.

Time for reading the Scriptures, praying, and meditating at the Western Wall (also called the Wailing Wall) of Jerusalem. It is one of the most sacred sites that remain from King Solomon's Temple, which was destroyed by the Babylonians in 586 B.C. and again by the Romans in A.D. 70. Jews from all over the world come to the Western Wall to commemorate the destruction of the Temple in the Fast of Tisha b'Ar - ninth day of the month of Ar-August. (Courtesy of BOAC)

CHRISTIANITY

The Cross:
Symbol of love

This my commandment:
That you love one another
As I have loved you.

John 15:12

CHRISTIANITY

The story of Christianity is the story of a religion that took root within the framework of Judaism in Palestine but very quickly spread, first eastward into Persia, then northward into Asia Minor, later westward into Europe, and finally throughout the globe. Early in its history, the Christian religion embraced on equal terms many converts from Jewish, Greek and Roman cultures; almost from the beginning its nature and scope was thought to be "universal" and not restricted to any particular group.

Hence, as it spread, the Christian religion absorbed and adopted a large number of elements and practices from Judaic, Hellenic, Roman and other religious sources. Weekly assemblies for regular "Sabbath" services was a practice inherited from Judaic tradition. From the Greek culture Christian scholars learned the art of logical argument and the expression of philosphical ideas; from Roman culture Christians borrowed the model of a centralized authority of law and order, and adapted it to fit an organized self-governing religious body: the church.

However, Christianity experienced many reverses during its process of expansion. Despite the teaching of universal love by its founder, Jesus, constant disputes, schisms (divisions), heresies and even wars marked (and still mark) the complicated and turbulent history of Christianity. Paradoxically, man persists in committing in the name of Jesus deeds directly opposed to his teaching. But first, who was Jesus and what was his teaching?

Jesus

Jesus was born around 4 B.C. to Joseph and Mary of the town of Nazareth in Galilee. An error in making the calendar accounts for this date, since the beginning of the Christian Era is usually assumed to date from the birth of Jesus. It was not until the sixth century A.D. that a Christian Roman monk divided history into *Before Christ* (B.C.) and *Anno Domini* (A.D.), Latin for in the Year of our Lord, in order to relate Christ's birth to the ancient Roman Calendar. However, his miscalculation, traditionally accepted by the Church and hallowed by long use, is too well established to be changed.

Very little is known about the childhood of Jesus except for incidents described in ancient legends. One of the most popular tells how Jesus, as a little boy, once amused himself by modelling clay images of sparrows. Delighted with his work, he clapped his hands, whereupon the little clay birds started to fly. During the fourth to sixth century A.D. when the sacred books of the New Testament were selected from among the many written materials, several "gospels" were omitted, partly because they contained such legendary stories about Jesus.

Two of the Gospels, Mark and John, make no mention at all of Jesus' virgin birth, childhood or youth. On the other hand, two of the Gospels, Matthew and Luke, declare that Jesus was born of a virgin and that supernatural events occurred at the time of his birth. Luke then goes on to describe Jesus' circumcision rite when he was eight days old and his learned conversation with the Jewish Rabbis in the Temple at Jerusalem when he was twelve years old. Mark's writings imply that Jesus' trade, like that of his father, was carpentry and that he had a number of brothers and sisters (Mark 6:3). Scarcely any more than this is known of his early years.

When Jesus was about thirty years old there appeared in Galilee a stern Jewish ascetic called John the Baptist. He announced the coming judgement of God and the preparation for the Messiah (Anointed One of God). Of course, many Jews expected such a Messiah who would deliver them from Roman rule. There had been many claimants to the title who briefly attracted a small band of followers before they were ruthlessly suppressed by the Romans. Some of the Jewish people may have been somewhat sceptical when John stood by the banks of the Jordan River and proclaimed, "Repent! For the Kingdom of Heaven is coming!" Many of them, including Jesus, were baptized by John. This incident marked the turning point in Jesus' life.

> When he came out of the water, immediately he saw the heavens opened and the Spirit descending upon him like a dove,

and a voice came from heaven, "Thou art my beloved Son; with thee I am well pleased."

Mark 1:10-11

This personal experience, a "call" directly from the "beyond", seems to have been shared by most great religious leaders: Moses and the voice from the burning bush, Mohammed and the voice in the cave outside Mecca, Paul and the voice on the Damascus road, Jesus and the voice by the Jordan River.

Jesus had to withdraw to a solitary place, the wilderness beyond Jordan, before finally deciding his future career. What actually happened during his forty days in the wilderness is a mystery. The Gospel of Mark says simply that he was there for forty days with the wild beasts and that the angels ministered to him (Mark 1:13). But Matthew and Luke record that Satan appeared in person and presented three temptations:

> And the tempter came and said to him, "If you are the Son of God, command these stones to become loaves of bread." But he answered, "It is written, 'Man shall not live by bread alone, but by every word that proceeds from the mouth of God.'"
>
> Then the devil took him to the holy city, and set him on the pinnacle of the temple, and said to him, "If you are the Son of God, throw yourself down; for it is written, 'He will give his angels charge of you,' and 'On their hands they will bear you up, lest you strike your foot against a stone.'" Jesus said to him, "Again it is written, 'You shall not tempt the Lord your God.'" Again, the devil took him to a very high mountain, and showed him all the kingdoms of the world and the glory of them; and he said to him, "All these I will give you, if you will fall down and worship me." Then Jesus said to him, "Begone, Satan! for it is written, 'You shall worship the Lord your God and him only shall you serve.'" Then the devil left him, and behold, angels came and ministered to him.

Matthew 4:3-11

Behind the imagery of this passage lies a significant issue which is raised in the words of the tempter: "If you are the Son of God. . . ." At the moment of baptism Jesus had heard a voice say, "Thou art my beloved Son. . . ." If there was any doubt in his mind that God had called him for a mission, it must have disappeared, for when Jesus came out of the wilderness he returned to Galilee and repeated John's message: "Repent ye, for the Kingdom of God is near!"

Gradually Jesus gathered about himself a group of twelve who constantly accompanied him on his preaching tours. Several of these disciples were fishermen, some were artisans, while one was a despised tax collector. In the meantime, news reached him that John the Baptist had been seized and put in prison. He carried on as if nothing had happened, travelling from place to place proclaiming the gospel (good news) of the Kingdom of God.

At first Jesus spoke in the Jewish synagogues, but when the crowds grew too large, he resorted to the open fields and market places. A full description of what happened in the synagogue on a Sabbath day is recorded in the first chapter of Mark. Accustomed to hearing the rabbis discuss the Torah and the Tradition, the people who heard Jesus were "astonished at his teaching, for he taught them as one who had authority, and not as the scribes" (Mark 1:22). But what amazed them most was the startling incident that interrupted the service and Jesus' speech. A member of the crowd, someone who is described as possessed "with an unclean spirit", must have sensed change in the usual order of service, and suddenly cried out: "What have you to do with us, Jesus of Nazareth? Have you come to destroy us? I know who you are – the holy one of God!" (Mark 1:24). Jesus reacted so powerfully that he silenced the heckler. The excited worshippers hailed the incident as a "miracle".

After the service, Jesus went to the home of Simon Peter, one of his new disciples, where Simon's mother-in-law was so sick that she could not get out of bed. Mark tells us that the fever left her as soon as Jesus took her hand and lifted her up. This incident strengthened his reputation as a healer. By sunset on that Sabbath day a crowd of sick people had gathered at the door and, according to Mark, many were cured (Mark 1:32-34).

Although the events recorded in the Gospels establish Jesus' reputation for healing, his authoritative personality and forceful speeches also brought him a large following. His compassion for people, especially the sick, the poor, the maimed and the blind; his love and understanding for children; and above all his imaginative use of parables; attracted the crowds during the early part of his ministry. He illustrated complex ideas by reference to everyday objects and incidents. He adapted his teaching to his audience; he made his teaching relevant. A number of his parables are regarded as literary classics: "The Prodigal Son" (Luke 15:11-32), "The Ninety Nine and One Lost Sheep" (Luke 15:3-7) and "The Good Samaritan" (Luke 10:30-37).

However, Jesus also invited serious opposition by challenging time-honoured assumptions. He sternly rebuked those who professed to be religious but were insincere and hypocritical (Matthew 6:1-22;23). His easy relations with people of all types – farmers, fishermen, and social outcasts such as tax collectors and prostitutes – reveal his impartiality and his indifference to social barriers and prejudices (Matthew 9:10-11). He ignored a number of the Jewish Traditions and scorned those who had substituted social and ceremonial practices for inward morality (Matthew 9). External features of "moral" behaviour were less important to Jesus than man's inward motivation – the spirit behind the action (Mark 7:1-23). Morality, according to Jesus, did not depend upon correct forms but upon one's attitude towards justice, mercy and integrity. Complacency, pride, the desire to achieve material success and status, self-centredness, and hypocrisy result from immoral social and religious values (Matthew 23). No wonder there arose a serious threat to his life.

Jesus' career as a preacher and teacher lasted only a year or two before he, like John the Baptist, was arrested and put to death. Although the reasons for the trial and execution of Jesus are puzzling and not altogether clear, the evidence clearly indicates that Jesus met his death on the cross like any other criminal or rebel under the Roman

Pilgrims in Jerusalem in procession along the Via Dolorossa - the traditional way to Calvary. (Courtesy of BOAC)

administration. The picture portrayed in the Gospels of Jesus preparing his disciples for his approaching death, reminds one of the Greek philosopher Socrates and his death. Each man knew that his life was soon to end, but for each death was incidental.

As it turned out, however, the death of Jesus was no more than a prelude to new insights and a new quality of experience among his followers. No one could have imagined at the time that anyone living for little more than thirty years, all but the last year or two in comparative obscurity, would win the allegiance of such vast numbers of people. In fact, the events that followed the death of Jesus were of greater importance to the early Christian than the events that preceded it. Difficult as it may be to explain or understand the resurrection and the appearances of Jesus after his death, there is no doubt that his resurrection was real to his disciples. True, Jesus appeared only to those who were his former followers or associates, not to Romans nor to the Jewish public. But it seems unlikely that these disciples would have accepted martyrdom for the sake of a story they had made up.

No matter what hypothesis may be offered to explain the resurrection, the early disciples were convinced of the continued power and presence of Jesus. Two other incidents, recorded in the Book of Acts, confirmed their assurance and confidence that their leader had in a mysterious way risen.

> And when he [Jesus] had said this, as they were looking on, he was lifted up, and a cloud took him out of their sight. And while they were gazing into heaven as he went, behold two men stood by them in white robes, and said, "Men of Galilee, why do you stand looking into heaven? This Jesus, who was taken up from you into heaven, will come in the same way as you saw him go into heaven."
>
> Acts 1:9-11

The second incident happened some fifty days after Jesus' crucifixion, on the day of Pentecost, the Jewish Harvest Festival:

> When the day of Pentecost had come, they were all together in one place. And suddenly a sound came from heaven like the rush of a mighty wind, and it filled all the house where they were sitting. And there appeared to them tongues as of fire, distributed and resting on each one of them. And they were all filled with the holy spirit and began to speak in other tongues, as the Spirit gave them utterance.
>
> Acts 2:1-4

The early Christians did not know how to express adequately their admiration and praise of their leader but they attributed "godhood" to him and proclaimed him to be the "only begotten Son of God".

> For God so loved the world that he gave his only Son, that whoever believes in him should not perish but have eternal life.
>
> John 3:16

Little did the early Christians realize that their message was to affect mankind so deeply. Based on the few years of association with Jesus, the disciples went about spreading the stories of Jesus – what he did and what he taught. As the number of believers increased, churches were established and it became necessary to record the sayings and doings of Jesus for circulation among believers.

Naturally, many writings and collections of stories circulated widely during the first four to five hundred years of the history of the Christian church. Eventually, a number of writings (twenty-seven in total) were selected and assembled to form the New Testament. The New Testament is, of course, the primary source of information concerning Jesus and his teachings, as well as of the religious outlook of the early Christian community.

The Holy Scriptures

Of all the major living religions, Christianity is the only one that reveres and includes the whole scripture of another religion with its own sacred writings. Buddhism, which split from Hinduism, created its own scriptures and ignored the Hindu writings. The same exclusiveness is characteristic of Islamic scriptures. But Christianity made the Jewish Bible its own by placing it on an exact level with the distinctive books of Christian believers.

The sacred books of Judaism are called by Christians the Old Testament, suggesting the "Old Covenant" made with God by Moses at Mount Sinai. Following the saying in Jeremiah (31:31-34) and in Luke (22:20), the early Christians added the Old Testament to the New Testament, meaning the "New Covenant" made by Jesus with his disciples at the Last Supper. Both the Old Testament and the New Testament books constitute the sacred writings of Christianity, commonly referred to as The Holy Bible or The Holy Book, from *biblos*, the Greek word for "book".

Since the Old Testament books are described in the unit on Judaism, it is only necessary to mention that the Bible includes a number of disputed books (some fourteen writings) called the Apocrypha, sometimes sandwiched between the Old and New Testaments. The word *apocrypha* is a Greek term meaning "hidden" (books) and was first applied to books to be kept away from the public because of their esoteric nature. However, at a later date, the term came to signify "heretical" books. These books written by Jews between 200 B.C. and A.D. 100 have been the subject of controversy among Jews and Christians alike, who have never been able to decide whether the books of the Apocrypha are as sacred as the other books in the Bible.

The books of the New Testament were written between the years A.D. 50 to 100 and tell of the beginning of Christianity. The four Gospels (Matthew, Mark, Luke and John) record the life and teachings of Jesus. Then comes the book known as the Acts of the Apostles that records the history of the early Christian movement. Following the book of Acts are a number of Epistles (meaning letters) which are addressed either to individuals (such as the letters to Timothy) or to Christian groups (such as the letters to the Corinthians). Lastly, there is a visionary account of the final triumph of God in the book called Revelation.

The New Testament has been a decisive factor in shaping Western civilization. Although it is impossible to examine in a few pages all the views recorded in the New Testament, an attempt is made here to

Years of study and preparation are required before a person assumes ecclesiastical responsibilities. Here, monks are studying the scriptures in the monastery of New Norcia, Australia. (Courtesy of Australian News and Information Bureau)

consider the basic concepts and teachings of the founder, Jesus, and the thoughts of some of his followers.

Man's Relationship with God

From the time of his baptism by John the Baptist to the end of his short life, the reality of God occupied the central place in the thoughts of Jesus. His own intimate relationship with God deeply impressed his disciples as he strongly emphasized the fatherhood of God. He regarded every human being as more than just a creature or servant of God – man was a child of God. With profound assurance he stressed the paternal character of God and taught his followers to address God not in the traditional form of "O God, Our Lord", but as "Our Father".

> Our Father who art in heaven,
> Hallowed be they name.
> Thy kingdom come,
> Thy will be done,
> On earth as it is in heaven . . .
>
> Matthew 6:9-11

Of course, the fatherhood concept of God did not originate with Jesus. The prophets within Judaism had spoken of God's paternal nature. "For thou . . . O Lord, art our Father," says Isaiah, "our Redeemer from of old is thy name" (Isaiah 63:16). However, Judaism had always tended to portray God as the majestic, all-powerful, sovereign being who reigned and ruled supreme. There was no other god except God, and to approach him, one addressed him in prayer very formally: "O Lord, our God . . . " Jesus' concept of God is illustrated by the personal and intimate relationship with God implied by the terms Jesus used to address him. Jesus spoke of "my Father" and "your Father".

In reading the Gospels, one can immediately sense the remarkable closeness and intimate association that Jesus had with God. When the seventy disciples returned from their mission and related their successful ministry, Jesus rejoiced and on the spot proclaimed:

> I thank thee, Father, Lord of Heaven and earth, that thou hast hidden these things from the wise and understanding and revealed them to babes: Yes, Father, For such was thy gracious will.
>
> Luke 10:21

When the final hours of his life on this earth were approaching, Jesus celebrated the great annual Passover feast with his disciples for the last time and spoke to them after this last supper. The Gospel of John (chapters 14 to 17) gives us a vivid account of what Jesus spoke about. It is here (John 14-17) that Jesus reveals not only his deep relationship and intimacy with the Father, but how this relationship signifies to him complete union or oneness with the Father:

> . . . if you had known me, you would have known my Father . . .
>
> . . . He who has seen me has seen the Father . . .
>
> . . . I am in the Father and the Father in me . . .
>
> John 14:7,9,11

Nevertheless, "the Father is greater than I," said Jesus, and "I do as the Father has commanded me . . . " (John 14:28-31). Then suddenly he stopped and prayed:

> Father the hour has come;
> glorify thy Son that the Son may glorify thee . . .
> Holy Father, keep them [disciples] in thy name
> which thou hast given me, that they may be one,
> even as we are one . . .
> Now I am coming to thee . . .
> O righteous Father, the world has not known thee,
> but I have known thee . . .
>
> John 17:1

Touched by Jesus' insight and prayer, the disciples followed him to the Garden of Gethsemane. Deeply distressed and full of sorrow, Jesus fell to the ground and earnestly prayed once again:

> Abba, Father, all things are possible to thee; remove this cup from me; yet not what I will, but what thou wilt.
>
> Mark 14:32-36

When finally Jesus was crucified between two criminals, his close relationship with God is once again revealed by his words:

> Father, forgive them; for they know not what they do.
>
> Luke 23:34

His last words on the cross were,

> Father, into thy hands I commit my spirit!
>
> Luke 23:46

This personal closeness with the Father was the characteristic feature of Jesus' teaching. In fact, he taught that God was *everyone's* Father and that every person could communicate directly and intimately with him, regardless of place or time. "Beware of practising your piety before men in order to be seen by them," said Jesus, "For then you will have no reward from *your* Father who is in heaven" (Matthew 6:1).

Prayer, almsgiving, and fasting were not simply techniques for securing good public opinion but ways of developing personal involvement with one's Father:

> Thus, when you give alms, sound no trumpet before you, as the hypocrites do in the synagogues and in the streets, that they may be praised by men. Truly, I say to you, they have their reward. But when you give alms, do not let your left hand know what your right hand is doing, so that your alms may be in secret; and your Father who sees in secret will reward you.
>
> And when you pray, you must not be like the hypocrites; for they love to stand and pray in the synagogues and at the street corners, that they may be seen by men. Truly, I say to you, they have their reward. But when you pray, go into your room and shut the door and pray to your Father who is in secret; and your Father who sees in secret will reward you . . .
>
> And when you fast, do not look dismal, like the hypocrites, for they disfigure their faces that their fasting may be seen by men. Truly, I say to you, they have their reward. But when you fast, anoint your head and wash your face, that your fasting may not be seen by men but by your Father who is in secret; and your Father who sees in secret will reward you.
>
> Matthew 6:2-18

The disciples of Jesus sensed that there was something incommunicable about the conscious experience of the ever-present Father within Jesus. It seemed to them that Jesus saw himself completely unified in personality and attitude with God the Father. The intimacy of Jesus' communion with the Father was so obvious to them, yet so difficult to understand, that they felt stunned and bewildered. Nevertheless, this religious consciousness of Jesus soon sunk into their own consciousness as well. Peter, in the opening remarks of his letter states, "Blessed be the God and Father of our Lord Jesus. . . . " (Peter 1:3). Similarly Paul begins his letters by saying, "Grace to you and peace from God our Father . . . " (Romans 1:7, I Corinthians 1:3; Galatians 1:3; Ephesians 1:2; Phillipians 1:2; Colossians 1:2; I Thessalonians 1:1).

Jesus not only made all who heard him distinctly aware of their relationship with God, but directed their attention to the coming Kingdom of God which he referred to as the "Kingdom of Heaven". (See Matthew, chapters 13, 18 – 21 for parables of the Kingdom.) "The Kingdom of heaven may be compared to . . . " was the way Jesus began much of his teaching about God's Kingdom. His analogies regarding the Kingdom covered a wide range of everyday activities that everyone could understand.

> The Kingdom of heaven is like a grain of mustard seed which a man took and sowed in his field; it is the smallest of all seeds, but when it has grown, it is the greatest of shrubs and becomes a tree, so that the birds of the air come and make nests in its branches.
>
> The Kingdom of heaven is like leaven which a woman took and hid in three measures of meal, till it was all leavened.
>
> The Kingdom of heaven is like a treasure hidden in a field, which a man found and covered up; then in his joy he goes and sells all that he has and buys that field.
>
> Again, the Kingdom of heaven is like a merchant in search of fine pearls, who, on finding one pearl of great value, went and sold all that he had and bought it.
>
> Again, the Kingdom of heaven is like a net which was thrown into the sea and gathered fish of every kind; when it was full, men drew it ashore and sat down and sorted the good into vessels but threw away the bad. So it will be at the close of the age. The angels will come out and separate the evil from the righteous.
>
> Matthew 13:31-49

Whatever else Jesus may have implied by teaching about the Kingdom of heaven this much is certain; he urged all men to seek primarily the Kingdom of God and His righteousness.

Therefore do not be anxious, saying "What shall we eat?" or "What shall we drink?" or "What shall we wear?" . . . Your heavenly Father knows that you need them all. But seek first his kingdom and his righteousness, and all these things shall be yours as well.

Matthew 6:31-33

Jesus assured his hearers that God as a Father cared for every individual; no person was unworthy of receiving the Father's grace. Moreover, no person was to be excluded from the kingdom of heaven, for it was accessible to all who asked.

Ask, and it will be given to you;
seek, and you will find;
knock, and it will be opened to you.
For every one who asks receives,
and he who seeks finds
and to him who knocks it will be opened.

Matthew 7:7-8

Man's relationship with God is reasonably clear from the teachings of Jesus. What is less clear is how Jesus saw himself in relationship to God. Did he think of himself as a "child" or "son of God" in the same sense as he taught that everyone was a "child" or "son" of God? Or did he consider himself to be "The Son of God" in a very special sense? Did he regard himself as the Messiah (the Lord's anointed) or was it his disciples who later thought of him as the Messiah?

Obviously these questions have represented, and still represent, the knottiest issues of interpretation in the history of Christianity. And perhaps such crucial problems can never be finally answered. Nevertheless, one thing is beyond doubt: Jesus knew that he was "commissioned" or "sent" to proclaim the Kingdom and the Fatherhood of God (Luke 4:16-21; 43). Hence, he could choose twelve men to communicate to them something of his experience; he could go around healing and teaching with a moral assurance and decisive authority that impressed his followers.

He did not impress everybody. His ability and eloquence must have offended certain Jewish religious leaders, for soon the rumour spread that Jesus was "possessed" by the "prince of demons" (Mark 3:21-26). But whatever other people might think of him the central reality in Jesus' life (the ultimate reality of all life, according to Jesus) was the consciousness of the ever-present Father. Thus Jesus compared man's relationship to God to the relationship which normally exists in a loving family between a son and his father but he made it clear that the relationship between man and God is even closer and more intimate than any love between son and father. Man's ultimate purpose was to earnestly seek God's kingdom and His will on earth:

> Our Father who art in heaven,
> Hallowed be thy name.
> Thy kingdom come,
> Thy will be done,
> On earth as it is in heaven . . .

Matthew 6:9-11

Man's Relationship to Man

The teachings of Jesus centred around two concepts: the *Fatherhood* of God and the *brotherhood* of all men. Just as the Father loves all men even so must man love his fellow man. He proclaimed that the Father's love for man is so great and boundless that it is not governed by man's goodness or wickedness. God manifests his love and mercy to all men – both good and bad – without regard to need or merit. In other words, God loves you and me whether or not we need, want or even deserve His love. Hence, Jesus taught that man ought to love his fellow man in the same way, without exceptions and without conditions.

> If you love those who love you, what credit is that to you? For even sinners love those who love them. And if you do good to those who do good to you, what credit is that to you? For even sinners do the same. And if you lend to those from whom you hope to receive, what credit is that to you? Even sinners lend to sinners, to receive as much again.
>
> But love your enemies, and do good, and lend, expecting nothing in return; and your reward will be great, and you will be sons of the Most High; for he [God] is kind to the ungrateful and selfish.

Luke 6:32-36

The keynote of Jesus' teaching is expressed in the last two lines. Man's relationship to man must match God's relationship to man. Jesus insisted that in order to be called the "son of God" one ought to love one's enemies as much as one's friends.

You have heard that it was said, "You shall love your neighbour and hate your enemy." But I say to you, love your enemies and pray for those who persecute you, so that you may be sons of your Father who is in heaven; for he makes his sun rise on the evil and on the good, and sends rain on the just and on the unjust. For if you love those who love you, what reward have you? . . . Do not even the Gentiles do the same? You therefore must be perfect, as your heavenly Father is perfect.

Matthew 5:43-48

Jesus taught that the two concepts, the Fatherhood of God and the brotherhood of mankind, are inseparable. An individual who experiences an intimate fellowship with God the Father, must of necessity love mankind. Since it is the nature and character of the Father to love and be compassionate to all, then it follows that the "son" should reflect the nature of the Father (Luke 18:23-25). In fact, anyone who does not love mankind can know nothing about God, let alone be associated with him. To love the individual who is unjust, cruel, deceitful, ugly, and unloveable; to love the murderer, the social outcast and one's enemy as much as the good and the loveable, is to love God. To feed the hungry, to clothe the naked, to welcome the stranger, to cheer the sick, to visit the imprisoned – in short to love and serve man is to love and serve the Father (Matthew 25:24-46).

This teaching of Jesus so impressed the minds of many that an expert in Judaic Law (the Torah) once asked Jesus to explain what he meant by "loving one's neighbour as oneself" (Luke 10:29-37). Jesus replied by telling the story of a man who was robbed, beaten, stripped and left to die on the road. A priest and a teacher, who happened to pass that way, saw the man but ignored him and travelled on. A Samaritan (one of the group regarded as traditional enemies by Jews at that time) who was the next traveller to pass, pitied the man, stopped, helped him and took care of all his needs.

"Which of these three," said Jesus, "do you think, proved neighbour to the man who fell among the robbers?

"The one who showed mercy to him."

"Then go and do likewise," said Jesus.

Not only did Jesus teach that one must love one's fellow man, but he himself frequently associated with people who were considered outcasts and undesirables (Matthew 9:10-13). On one occasion, certain religious authorities questioned his association with such people and his attitude to them; he answered by quoting from their own scriptures:

Go and learn what this means,
"I desire mercy and not sacrifice!"

Matthew 9:13

Undoubtedly, they recognized and understood the significance of his reply. The quotation was from The Prophets (Hosea 6:6), where God expresses his preference for compassion among men rather than for sacrifices.

> On another occasion, some of the religious leaders came to Jesus with a woman caught in adultery. "Teacher, this woman has been caught in the act of adultery. Now in the Law (Torah), Moses commanded us to stone such, what do you say about her?"
>
> "Let him who is without sin among you be the first to throw a stone at her," replied Jesus.
>
> One by one the accusers turned away until only Jesus was left with the woman.
>
> "Woman, where are they? Has no one condemned you?"
>
> "No one, Lord,"
>
> Neither do I condemn you; go and do not sin again."

John 8:3-11

Although the scriptures sanctioned banishment of the guilty and the just settlement of every injustice, for Jesus the principle of love and mercy far outweighed any other. There was no question in his mind that the highest goal in life, the most valuable element in living, was *man's love to man,* irrespective of physical, social or religious standing. Man's purpose in life was to demonstrate God's nature: love, mercy and compassion to one and all.

This conviction of Jesus must have been so forceful that it gripped the minds of his followers, and its impact is felt very clearly in their writings:

> Beloved, let us love one another; for love is of God, and he who loves is born of God and knows God. He who does not love does not know God; for God is love . . .
>
> No man has ever seen God; if we love one another, God abides in us and his love is perfected in us . . .
>
> If any one says, "I love God," and hates his brother, he is a liar; for he who does not love his brother whom he has seen, cannot love God whom he has not seen.

I John 4:7-20

A classic definition of love and a very beautiful statement about it is found in chapter 13 of Paul's first letter to the people of Corinth.

> If I speak in the tongues of men and angels, but have not love, I am a noisy gong or a clanging cymbal. And if I have prophetic powers, and understand all mysteries and all knowledge; and if I have all faith, so as to remove mountains, but have not love, I am nothing. If I give away all I have, and if I deliver my body to be burned, but have not love, I gain nothing . . .
>
> I Corinthians 13:1-3

Paul was simply elaborating what Jesus had taught, a process begun by his disciples as soon as Jesus' mortal life ended on the cross, and continued to this day. One question still eludes us. What was Jesus' own view about man? Did he agree with some Jewish scholars of his day that since the time when Adam and Eve had been thrown out of the garden of Eden (Genesis 3) man was inherently evil, that he was "born in sin"? Is evil part of man's make-up, like lungs or the hair on his head?

Two of the Gospel writers (Luke and John) have nothing to say about this problem of man's original sin. The other two Gospel writers, however, (Matthew 15:1-20 and Mark 7:1-23) record a discussion among Jesus and certain religious authorities who questioned him regarding the Tradition of the elders.

> "Why do your disciples transgress the Tradition of the elders, and eat with hands defiled (ritually unwashed)?" they asked.
>
> "And why do you transgress the commandment of God for the sake of your Tradition?" Jesus asked.
>
> Then Jesus turned to all who were present there and said,
>
> "Hear me, all of you, and understand: not what goes into the mouth defiles a man, but what comes out of the mouth, this defiles a man."
>
> When his disciples showed by their questions that they didn't understand what he was talking about, Jesus went on to say,
>
> "Do you not see that whatever goes into a man from outside cannot defile him, since it enters not in his heart but his stomach, and so passes on? What comes out of a man is what defiles a man. For from within, out of the heart of man, come evil thoughts, fornication, theft, murder, adultery, coveting, wickedness, deceit, licentiousness, envy, slander, pride, foolishness. All these evil things come from within, and they defile a man."

Thus, Jesus declared that sin lies deep in the heart of man. It is what lies in the heart – the hidden attitudes and motives – rather than outward actions that should be judged. But his statement offers no explanation of the nature of sin. Nor does he mention anything about man's original sin. It may be that his idea of the nature of sin was similar to one of the then current Judaic concepts, but certainly he shows no interest in defining sin or its origin in the abstract sense.

Nevertheless, the presence and problem of sin is strongly emphasized in the New Testament, especially in the writings of Paul. It is helpful to consider the contribution of Paul, since many of his views shaped the future of Christianity and came to dominate the thinking of the Christian church.

Paul

At about the time when the disciples were proclaiming that they had seen Jesus after his death, a young Jew called Saul arrived in Jerusalem from Tarsus in Cilicia. He had travelled south to study under the most highly regarded Jewish Rabbis, the expert teachers of the day. There were no universities then and students travelled long distances to study under famous scholars.

Saul was well versed not only in the Jewish Law (the Torah and the Traditions), but in Greek culture as well. However, two incidents in his life changed his attitudes towards both Judaic Law and Hellenistic culture.

One of these incidents grew out of the courageous and enthusiastic preaching of the disciples who spoke about the resurrection and power of Jesus. The Roman Government could do nothing to stop what it regarded as a heretical movement. Arresting the members of this movement, beating them or imprisoning them had no effect upon them whatsoever. In fact, the persecution had quite the opposite effect from the authorities' intention. It forced the followers of the "Jesus" group to escape from Jerusalem into other districts and distant countries. Saul was aware of all this and one incident of persecution impressed him.

The persecutors had captured a young man named Stephen, who was accused of preaching heretical views (Acts 6:8 - 8.2). After being examined and condemned, he was led to the outskirts of the city, and there, according to the method of dealing with heretics in those times, he was stoned to death. A number of those who were hurling stones at Stephen left their "garments at the feet of a young man named Saul" (Acts 7:58).

After this incident, Saul volunteered to hunt down the followers of

Jesus. First, moving from house to house in Jerusalem he "dragged off men and women and committed them to prison" (Acts 8:3). Then, securing the necessary documents, he left Jerusalem for Damascus in order to root out the heretical Jesus movement. However, an incident on the road transformed his life (Acts 9:1-22).

> Now as he journeyed he approached Damascus, and suddenly a light from heaven flashed about him. And he fell to the ground and heard a voice saying to him, "Saul, Saul, why do you persecute me?" And he said, "Who are you, Lord?" And he [the voice] said, "I am Jesus, whom you are persecuting; but rise and enter the city, and you will be told what you are to do."
> Acts 9:3-6

Here is something analogous to the prophetic experiences of Judaism, except that the focus of the experience is not God but Jesus. Moses, Isaiah, Jeremiah, and all the ancient Judaic prophets had heard the voice of God. So had Jesus. But Paul's focus of experience shifted from the voice of God to the voice of Jesus. And in subsequent centuries, the Christian church adopted this shift of emphasis, centering all its doctrines (principles of belief) and theological views on Jesus.

It was from this experience on the road to Damascus that Saul's new purpose in life emerged. He not only stopped persecuting the followers of the Jesus sect, but he became the foremost advocate of the movement and began his mission to convert the world he knew to Christ. Not only did he change his name from Saul to Paul; he also reversed all his former views. He saw in the resurrected Jesus (who spoke with him) the answer to many of his personal problems. In the course of his daily activities he evolved his own distinctive religious beliefs.

In Paul's view, Jesus, through his resurrection, had brought a new freedom which made strict adherence to the Torah and to the detailed Traditions unnecessary. It was useless, Paul argued, to attempt to gain God's favour by keeping the Law and Traditions. Man cannot be justified before God by his good works but by faith in Jesus Christ (Romans 3:20-22,28; 5:1; Galatians 2:16).

Paul travelled widely in the Roman Empire, preaching unceasingly this new freedom in Christ Jesus. He compared a Christian to an heir born into a rich estate. Man is born, through faith in Jesus Christ, into the full inheritance of the Kingdom of God. The chosen people of God were now not only the people of Israel, but all who through faith in Jesus became the children of God. Of course, this meant a liberation from the numerous regulations of the Torah, though Paul was quick to point out that this new freedom meant governing one's life by the principle of love (I Corinthians 13:1 - 14:1).

Naturally enough the non-Jewish converts raised no objections to Paul's ideas. These converts were under no obligation to accept Judaic regulations (in particular the rite of circumcision) in order to maintain their membership in the new Christian sect. But the Judaic Law became an issue which split the early Christian community into two groups. The "Judaizers" wished to keep the Christian movement within the rule of Judaic Law and Traditions, while the "Pauline" thinkers believed that Christianity should become liberal and open itself out to wider opportunities. The issue became so critical that a decision had to be made quickly. About A.D. 49, the first Christian Council was held in Jerusalem to discuss this matter. A number of disciples and leaders, including Paul, were at this meeting. After lengthy discussions, the following resolution was made:

> . . . to abstain from the pollutions of idols and from unchastity and from what is strangled and from blood.
>
> Acts 15:20

In the long and turbulent history of the Christian church, Paul's views and the views of his followers won out. Many modern scholars argue that Paul, rather than Jesus, should be regarded as the founder of Christianity. His influence was so powerful that in subsequent centuries Christians were more inclined to form their religious beliefs on the basis of his writings rather than on the Gospels.

Paul's teachings did not centre around God, but around the figure of Jesus the Christ. To him, Jesus was not just a man, but the one who had been resurrected by the power of God; hence he was called the Christ (from the Greek word *Christos* meaning "anointed one"). Jesus was the long promised and long awaited Messiah (a Hebrew word meaning "anointed one"). Unconcerned as he was with Jesus' birth, life, teachings and activities, the focal point of Paul's views and teachings was the crucifixion and resurrection of Jesus. Unlike Jesus, Paul was very specific in his views on original sin. Man could be saved from his inherent sinful nature not by rigid adherence to the Torah but by identifying himself with the death and resurrection of Jesus in the rite of baptism (Romans 6:3-11).

The purpose of the Torah, according to Paul, was simply to show man his sinful nature in much the same way as a mirror reflects an image. The cause of death was sin, and Paul traced the origin of sin back to the transgression, or disobedience, of Adam, the father of mankind (Romans 5:12-21). This belief in original sin was not Paul's alone. It was one of many views then current in rabbinical circles; but it never won as much acceptance among Jews as it did among Christians. According to Paul's view, all men are sinners, not because of any personal wrong-doing, but because of an originally warped and infected nature. Only Christ can restore men, and Paul described how this could come about.

Christ's death was a self-sacrifice which atoned for the sin of mankind. Christ's resurrection was the proof of this atonement and the triumph over death, hence over sin. Just as Adam was representative of mankind, so is Christ. If through the act of one man – Adam – all men became sinners, then through the act of one man – Jesus – men may be restored to righteousness (Romans 5:18-19). But, whether or not *all* mankind may be "chosen" or may be saved seems questionable to Paul:

> For those whom he [God] foreknew he also predestined to be conformed to the image of his Son . . .
> And those whom he [God] predestined he also called; and those whom he called he also justified; and those whom he justified he also glorified.
>
> Romans 8:29-30

This speculation about the meaning of Jesus' death and resurrection raises more problems than it answers. What is Jesus' relationship with God and man? Is he to be considered a man or a God or is he partly God and partly man? Is he in some way a "creature of God" or did he emanate (issue, proceed) from God? Is he equal to God or subordinate to God? Moreover, are *all* men sinners and hopelessly lost without Jesus, even though their cultural and religious backgrounds may differ? Can *all* men become automatically justified through Christ's death and resurrection as they are automatically born sinners through Adam?

More than 1900 years have passed and the questions have not yet been settled. Throughout this period the pendulum of thought has constantly swung from one extreme to another, dividing the Christian church into numerous sects and denominations. Of course, as Christianity spread out from its Judaic environment into the Graeco-Roman world, it was inevitable that it should face many new problems. Let us then trace briefly the history of Christianity in order to understand its present state.

The Development of Christianity

The first few centuries were critical times for Christianity. From its beginning, a series of persecutions threatened its survival, but after struggling through various severe conflicts and adopting a number of different religious patterns, it finally won a tremendous triumph. In the early fourth century A.D., Christianity was declared by the Emperor Constantine to be the Imperial State religion of Rome. But what are the highlights of the first four centuries?

Christianity emerged from the heart of Judaism, but very quickly included non-Jewish converts. Hence, the members of the early church represented elements from many cultures: Judaic, Greek, Roman, and a number of other cultures as well. Naturally, the Christians adopted a number of traditions that belonged to the various cultural groups. Not only did the new converts to Christianity quarrel among themselves, but the majority of Jews, Greeks and Romans viewed the converts as traitors who threatened the old traditions and beliefs. The Christians were divided by the ways in which they interpreted the teachings of Jesus. The rest of the world was united against them by common fear and hatred.

Orthodox Jews distrusted the Christians because the Christians borrowed part of Jewish tradition, changing it to suit their new religion. At least three basic traditional elements were carried over from Judaism into Christianity and altered in form. First, the Judaic rite of circumcision as the sign of the convenant was replaced by the rite of baptism as the sign of the new covenant. Then, the Judaic weekly tradition of the Sabbath service was modified by the regular weekly service on Sunday, commemorating the day of Jesus' resurrection. At this service scriptures were read and instruction given in the Judaic tradition, but unlike Judaism, the *shekinah* (divine presence) was replaced by the Eucharistic meal (Communion, or the Lord's Supper). Third, though the importance of the Judaic scriptures was recognized and accepted, Christian interpretation differed from Judaic thought. All these factors created tremendous friction between Judaism and Christianity.

Orthodox Judaism regarded the Christian movement as heterodox (heretical), because converted Jews claimed that an imposter – Jesus – was the long-awaited Messiah. Moreover, these converts claimed that Jesus could forgive sins and was one with God. Such a statement was blasphemy to orthodox Judaism. Besides, many Jews, like Paul, declared that strict adherence to the Torah and Traditions was unnecessary since faith in Christ was the only way to gain righteousness and justification in the sight of God. There was constant trouble between orthodox Jew and Christian until the gap seemed irreconcilable.

Hellenistic (Greek) culture also played a role in the development of Christianity. The common language in the Eastern Roman Empire, (outside Palestine and the neighbouring countries) was Greek. Not only was it a widespread language, but it was a language that was able to express philosophical views very subtly and convey profound religious thought in poetry. Hence, Christianity inherited the art of logical thinking from the Hellenic culture. Nevertheless, Christians also came into sharp conflict with the Greeks.

Whenever there was a natural calamity, such as an earthquake, a fire, an epidemic or a disaster the Greeks explained it as the vengeance of their gods against the Christians. Hence, they persecuted the Christians, blaming them for such disasters. In the long run, however, Christians succeeded in eradicating the rich Hellensitic religion and philosophy. "The gods of Greece really perished," says a modern scholar, "perished unwept and unmourned." What is more important though, is that with the death of the Greek gods the achievements of Greek philosophy died also.

Although the Roman contribution to Western civilization is incalculable, and although the church eventually inherited the Roman organizational pattern (a centralized government with a hierarchical structure), the Romans were the greatest early persecutors of Christianity. As early as A.D. 64, the Roman Emperor Nero was using Christian victims for the bloody Roman arenas. Christians joined the sad procession of slaves, prisoners and criminals who were condemned to burn at the stake or be mauled by lions for the public amusement of the Roman crowd. In order to stamp out the fast-spreading Christian movement, the Roman Emperors imposed ruthless measures. Accused of holding secret orgies, and charged with infanticide, incest, and cannibalism, Christians were tortured by crueller methods than can be imagined. The height of persecution came in A.D. 303, under the Emperor Diocletian, who, not content to torture Christians, burned their churches, destroyed their scriptures, and conducted an organized campaign of extermination.

And yet, less than ten years later, under the rule of the Emperor Constantine (A.D. 274-337), the entire picture changed. Not only did Constantine restore church property; he also built new church buildings to replace those that had been destroyed. Not only did Constantine grant Christians freedom of conscience and worship; he strongly supported the faith.

Despite intensive persecution and attempts at extermination, Christianity slowly spread into Egypt, North Africa, Persia, and as far as

India. Zoroastrianism, the dominant religion of the powerful Persian Empire, was just as intolerant of Christianity as the Romans. The Persians were determined to check the Christian movement within the Persian Empire. However, the internal disputes and heresies that now began to divide the Christians became far more of a threat to their survival than the persecutions they faced.

The Christian churches within the Roman Empire were confronted with a political division and a division by language. Diocletian, Constantine's predecessor, had divided the Roman Empire into an Eastern and a Western province. Rome, in the western province, was the capital of the entire Empire and an important Christian centre; Latin was the dominant language. On the other hand, in the Eastern province there were a number of other important Christian centres (such as Antioch and Alexandria), and the dominant language was Greek.

Once Constantine had legalized Christianity within the entire Roman Empire, he resolved to establish (in A.D. 324) a rival capital in the Eastern province on the site of Byzantium – known until recently as Constantinople, the city (Greek *polis*) of Constantine.

Constantinople became as important a centre as Rome in the history of Christianity. Inevitably the two centres competed for the leadership of the Christian church. The rivalry between Constantinople and Rome (Eastern Christendom versus Western Christendom) persisted till A.D. 1054, when finally the two severed their relationship completely. Through the centuries, one was referred to as the Roman Catholic Church (Latin-speaking) and the other as the Eastern Orthodox Church (Greek-speaking).

Perhaps, however, the greatest influence for good or for evil that Constantine exerted on the development of Christianity was to convene the first "Ecumenical Council" in A.D. 325. He thus established a precedent by uniting church and state, with the state taking the initiative.

At his own expense, Constantine convened this Council of 300 bishops from all over the Roman Empire at a place called Nicaea to settle two major controversies which were shaking the foundations of the Eastern churches. One was the date of Easter and the other was a theological dispute (commonly referred to as "Arianism") between Arius, an old priest, and his Bishop Alexander, who were both from the church in Alexandria, Egypt. The first question, the date of Easter, was easily resolved, but the second question proved difficult. The issue was a fundamental matter which concerned the nature of Jesus in relation to God.

Whereas Arius and his followers maintained that Jesus and the Holy Spirit had a subordinate position in relation to God, Alexander and his group regarded Jesus as "God of God . . . being of one substance with the Father". The deliberations of the assembly resulted in a statement of belief:

The Nicene Creed

I believe in one God, the Father almighty, maker of heaven and earth, and of all things visible and invisible. And in one Lord Jesus Christ, the only-begotten Son of God. Born of the Father before all ages. God of God, light of light, true God of true God. Begotten not made; being of one substance with the Father, by whom all things were made, who for us men, and for our salvation, came down from heaven. And was incarnate by the Holy Ghost of the Virgin Mary . . . And I believe in the Holy Ghost the Lord and giver of life; who proceedeth from the Father and the Son. Who together with the Father and the Son is adored and glorified . . .

Monasteries house people who live in seclusion from the world, assume religious vows, and follow a fixed rule. Here, monks are taking a leisurely walk in the monastery grounds of New Norcia, Australia. (Courtesy of Australian News and Information Bureau)

This statement of belief established Christianity's concept of Jesus' divinity as well as the status of the Trinity (Father, Son and Holy Ghost). But the immediate result was chaos: a battle within the churches began after the Nicene Creed was established. Christians denounced each other as heretics, condemned each other, banished each other, and often ruthlessly put each other to death.

Such unrest within the churches led to a second Ecumenical Council in Constantinople in A.D. 381, convened by the Emperor Theodosius I. However, attendance at the second Council was smaller than at the first (about 150), since it was restricted to the Bishops of the Eastern part of the Empire. Through the efforts of three outstanding Eastern Christian thinkers, known as the Coppadocian Fathers, a reconciliation was worked out and peace was restored to the churches.

The second Council established five important Ecclesiastical Provinces (four Eastern and one Western) and forbade the Patriarchs (leaders or heads) to interfere outside their boundaries:

ROME: whose jurisdiction extended over the entire Western half of the Roman Empire.

CONSTANTINOPLE: whose supervision extended over thirty-nine districts.

ALEXANDRIA: whose supervison extended over fourteen districts.

ANTIOCH: whose supervision extended over thirteen districts.

JERUSALEM: whose supervision extended over five districts.

The peace that prevailed in Eastern Christendom was temporary. Half a century after the second Council a third Ecumenical Council was called in Ephesus in A.D. 431 by the Emperor Theodosius II. The conflict was between the Patriarchs of Constantinople and Alexandria: Nestorius and Cyril respectively. The issue at stake was the nature of Jesus. The Patriarch of Alexandria and his supporters (which included the representatives from Rome) insisted that Jesus had *one* nature, at once divine and human. The Patriarch of Constantinople and his supporters claimed that Jesus had two natures, divine and human. Each Patriarch charged the other with heresy; each man solemnly excommunicated the other. Emperor Theodosius II accepted and confirmed both excommunications so that both Patriarchs were forced to resign.

The dispute remained unresolved and internal disharmony continued to drain the strength of the Eastern churches for almost two centuries, until Eastern Christendom received its first crippling blow. About the seventh century A.D. the new force of Islam swept eastward carrying all before it.

St. Basil's Cathedral in Red
Square, Moscow, built in
the sixteenth century, is an
example of an Eastern
Orthodox church. (Cour-
tesy of BOAC)

St. Peter's Basilica in Vatican City is the mother church of Catholicism and the largest
church in the world. The area, including the square, is believed to be the site of
Emperor Nero's circus where thousands of Christians suffered martyrdom. Tradition
has it also that St. Peter died here on a cross about A.D. 64 — hence the name, St.
Peter's Basilica. (Courtesy of Trans World Airlines)

In the meantime, the Roman Empire rapidly declined while Christendom steadily increased in strength. State and Church became more and more intertwined until ultimately Christian civilization emerged. In A.D. 1054, Christianity suffered its sharpest division when Eastern and Western Christendom separated permanently.

All these divisions seem far removed from the teachings of Jesus in the Gospels, and there were probably many people who tried to stop Christianity from becoming a destructive force. Their efforts were doomed to failure.

In A.D. 1095 Western Christendom (henceforth known as the Roman Catholic Church), under Pope Urban II, appealed to Christians to fight a "holy war" in order to regain Jerusalem, the Holy City, from the power of Islam. Thus the Crusades were inspired by the Church. The Crusades gave rise to so many acts of violence and barbarism that, if they could, most thinking people would gladly erase the scar that these wars left on the memories of all nations. One of the Crusades was directed against Eastern Christendom. On Good Friday, A.D. 1204, the Crusaders sacked Constantinople, dethroned the Patriarch, whose rank was equivalent to the Pope's in Rome, and replaced him with one who recognized the Roman Catholic Pope. Constantinople, the once-

St. Paul's Cathedral in London, built in the seventeenth century, is an example of a Protestant church. (Courtesy of BOAC)

great Eastern Christian centre, survived for two more centuries, but finally fell to the Turks in A.D. 1453.

The spirit of revolt was now in the air; voices of discontent were raised by many who urged a return to a simpler and purer religious life. Serious thinkers were questioning the power and authority of the Roman Church. Various religious practices were being appraised and criticized. The Roman Catholic Church resisted this pressure until, from within its own ranks, a movement emerged which split Western Christendom into two.

The chief figure in this movement was a German monk, Martin Luther. On October 31, 1517, he nailed his "Ninety-Five Theses" to the door of All Saints Church in Wittenberg. This document, which created a series of chain reactions, was the beginning of the Protestant Reformation. Just as the Eastern Church had separated from the Western Church in A.D. 1054, so now the followers of Protestantism separated themselves from the Roman Catholics. Northern Europe, notably Germany, Scandinavia and England, joined the Protestant movement; Southern Europe, especially Italy, France and Spain, remained Roman Catholic.

Though these were exciting times, they led to the most tragic inter-religious war in the history of Christianity: the Thirty Years' War. Europe was drenched in blood, as Protestants and Roman Catholics fought in the name of Christianity. The result was a spirit of intolerance and division; hence Protestantism divided into many denominations, and these in turn divided into many sects.

Religious intolerance of "heretics" was, of course, nothing new. From the thirteenth century onward, Western Christendom developed an organization called "The Inquisition" to fight heresy. It was a court to detect and punish those who held ideas opposed to the accepted views of the Church. Imprisonment, exile, physical torture, public burning, and a host of unspeakable horrors were inflicted upon men and women whose religious views differed from that of the Church. Paradoxically, while the Protestant movement was a movement of protesters, or protestants, against the interference of the Church, it was soon guilty of the same kind of interference and intolerance which Protestants had criticized in the Roman Catholic Church. It used the same methods of force in imposing its own views upon those believers who did not conform to the beliefs of a particular Protestant group.

After almost four centuries of hostility and continuous division into splinter groups, a remarkable change is taking place. There is a distinct trend towards religious toleration at the present time. Moreover, many efforts are being made toward the reunion of subdivisions as well as major branches of Christianity. The degree of cooperation among

Pope Paul blessing the crowds that line the streets of Sydney, Australia, on his way to the Pan-Oceania Episcopal Conference. In the background is the spire of St. James' Church, one of the oldest Anglican churches in Australia. At the left is a statue of Queen Victoria. (Courtesy of Australian News and Information Bureau)

denominations and religious groups with different points of view is so notable in modern times that men of good will everywhere wait impatiently for the day when human beings will join hands to fulfil great ideals and aspirations. There is an increasing tendency to discover in the other person virtues that were once denied or ignored in the blindness of intolerance.

Christianity as a whole is undergoing unprecedented changes. So swiftly and so widely are new developments occurring that the disillusionment of the past seems irrelevant to the promise of the future.

SOME OF THE MAIN PROTESTANT GROUPS

Adventist (Seventh Day Adventist)
Anglican (Episcopal in U.S.)
Baptist

Brethren
Christian Scientist
Church of God
Congregational
Disciples of Christ
Ethical Culture Movement
Evangelistic Associations
Jehovah's Witnesses
Latter-day Saints (Mormon)

Lutheran
Mennonite
Methodist (Oxford Movement)
Moravian
Old Catholic
Pentecostal
Presbyterian
Quaker (Friends)
Reformed
Salvation Army
Spiritualist
Universalist

RECENT MERGERS OF RELIGIOUS GROUPS

Date	Country	New merger name	Groups united
1925	Canada	United Church of Canada	Methodist, Congregational, Presbyterian
1938	France	Reformed Church of France	Reformed Church of France, Reformed Evangelical Church of France, Evangelical Methodist Church of France, Union of Evangelical Free Churches
1941	Japan	Church of Christ in Japan	Methodist, Presbyterian, Congregational, and 13 other denominations
1946	Netherlands	Dutch Reformed Church	Dutch Reformed Church, Reformed Churches in the Netherlands
1947	India	Church of South India	Presbyterian, Congregational, Methodist, Anglican
1948	Germany	Evangelical Church in Germany	Twenty-seven independent churches
1961	U.S.A.	United Church of Christ	Congregational, Evangelical, Reformed

ISLAM

The star and crescent moon:
Symbol of Islam

Allah is most great! Allah is most great!
I bear witness that there is no god but Allah!
I bear witness that Mohammed is the Apostle of Allah!
Come to prayer! Prayer is better than sleep!

ISLAM

The Islamic religion is the youngest of man's great universal religions and, in many ways, the simplest. Making its appearance early in the seventh century A.D., it developed with astonishing speed into a great cohesive civilization, extending all the way from the Atlantic Ocean to the borders of China. The birthplace of this compelling new faith was Arabia, then a semi-nomadic and semi-urban civilization.

The word *Islam* means "submission" and a *Muslim* is "one who submits" to the will of God. The origin of the Islamic religion lies either at the beginning of time, at creation, or in the sixth century A.D. in Arabia, depending upon the point of view one wishes to take. From the orthodox Muslim perspective, the story of Islam starts not with Mohammed, but shares a common tradition with Judaism and a common Biblical origin when God, or rather Allah, created the world and the first man, Adam. The descendants of Adam are traced to Noah, who had a son named Shem. This is where the word Semite – descendants of Shem – comes from; and like the Jews, Arabs regard themselves as a Semitic people. Shem's descendants are then traced to Abraham and to his wives Sarah and Hagar. At this point, two familiar stories about Abraham provide the cornerstones of the Islamic religion. The first, Abraham's attempted sacrifice of his son Isaac, demonstrates the submission of Abraham in the supreme test: hence the word "Islam". The second, concerning Ishmael's banishment, gave rise to the belief that Ishmael (the son of Abraham and Hagar) went to Mecca and that eventually from his descendants the prophet Mohammed emerged in the sixth century A.D.

Mohammed

Another point of view is that the Islamic religion began with its founder Mohammed. Mohammed was born in Mecca (circa A.D. 571) into the tribe of Quraish, whose members acted as custodians of a shrine called *Ka'aba*, meaning "cube". It was a rectangular structure that contained various idols. In one corner of the Ka'aba stood a black meteorite, believed to have streaked out of the heavens one night in the forgotten past. Mohammed's family supplied drinking water to the many pilgrims.

At that time the city of Mecca was a prosperous transfer point on the ancient trade route between India and the West, and the centre of religious pilgrimages. Camel caravans brought traders from many lands and Arab tribes came to worship at the city's numerous shrines. Though the most popular and respected shrine was the Ka'aba, the Meccans worshipped many deities, among whom was Allah. Capable of inspiring genuine religious devotion among his followers, Allah was regarded as creator, provider and determiner of man's destiny.

Tombstones and tragedy marked the course of Mohammed's early life. His father died a few days before his birth; his mother died when he was only six years old, and, three years later, his grandfather, who was taking care of him, died too. Finally, at the age of nine, he was entrusted to his paternal uncle, Abu Talib.

As a young man, Mohammed went into the caravan conducting business and at the age of twenty-five entered the service of a wealthy widow named Khadijah. Though she was fifteen years older than he was, her relationship with Mohammed deepened into love, until finally they married. This union must have relieved Mohammed of economic care and given him freedom to pursue his spiritual inclinations.

Mohammed's full ministry did not begin until fifteen years after his marriage. Through the years he had developed a distaste for the polytheistic worship of the desert Arabs and he must have pondered the monotheistic conception of the Jewish and Christian faiths. Often he wandered into the hills, especially into a cave outside Mecca, to seek solitude for his meditation.

It was on one such visit to the cave that Mohammed received his divine call (A.D. 610). Like Abraham, Moses, Samuel and Jesus, Mohammed heard a divine voice, which said, "Recite!" Overwhelmed by this voice and the appearance of the archangel Gabriel, Mohammed fell prostrate to the ground. The voice repeated, "Recite!" "What shall I recite?" asked Mohammed in terror. And the answer came:

> Recite – in the name of thy Lord who created!
> Created man from clots of blood!

Recite – for thy Lord is most beneficent,
who has taught the use of the pen;
has taught man that which he knew not!

Sura 96:1-4

Terrified by the overwhelming, divine presence, Mohammed rushed home and told Khadijah that he had either become "possessed" (mad), or a prophet. On hearing the full story, his wife encouraged him: "Rejoice and be of good cheer, thou wilt be the Prophet of this people!"

Like the Old Testament prophets, Mohammed was fired by an overwhelming desire to proclaim his revelations to his countrymen. He preached strongly on three issues: the oneness of Allah, the moral responsibility of man towards Allah, and the judgement awaiting mankind on the day of resurrection. It must be noted that Mohammed insisted, then and always, that he was not divine, but merely a man chosen to be the spokesman of Allah.

Despite abuse, ridicule and persecution, especially from the priests of the Ka'aba, Mohammed proceeded to preach against idolatry and called men to recognize the worship of Allah only. Like the Judaic prophets, Mohammed claimed for Allah the attribute they had claimed for God. Allah was not a god, or even the greatest of gods; Allah was what his name literally claimed: the One and Only God, without rival. It was this uncompromising monotheism that invited the hostility of the Meccans. Mohammed would have been killed but for the protection afforded by his uncle, who nevertheless begged him to abandon this form of teaching.

Meanwhile Mohammed's fame spread to neighbouring tribes and cities. One day a delegation suddenly came from Yathrib (later renamed Medina, from the Arabic *Medinat an Nabi*, meaning the "City of the Prophet", in honour of Mohammed), which was some 280 miles north of Mecca. This delegation invited him to come and mediate their tribal feuds and promised him protection. Mohammed and some of his disciples fled to Medina on September 24, A.D. 622. This migration is known in Arabic as the *Hegira* (meaning "flight") and is the year from which all Muslim calendars are dated. Moreover, the Hegira is regarded among Muslims as the turning point, not only in the development of Islam, but in world history as well.

Although the people of Medina were more interested in a political figure than in a religious leader, Mohammed quickly won over the inhabitants to his faith. He became the city's political chief as well as its religious leader. Thus, under his direction, civil and religious authority were fused. For the next ten years, until his death, Mohammed struggled to unite his countrymen into a coherent politico-religious group; and he succeeded. At the time of his death in A.D. 632 virtually all of Arabia was under his control. No other Arab had ever succeeded in uniting his countrymen as Mohammed had. Moreover, he had aroused the violent energies of his desert countrymen and now they had one consuming goal: the conquest and conversion of the world.

It must be remembered that, for Mohammed, and hence for all Muslims, service to the state was identical with service to Islam. Thus, immediately after Mohammed's death, the Arabs exploded upon the world. Within little more than a century after their prophet's death, the Arabs had extended their dominion from Spain to India.

The Qur'an

The sacred Scripture of the Islamic religion is the Qur'an. The Arabic word *Qur'an* means "recitation"; the beauty of the language is fully revealed when it is read aloud with specific intonations: an artistic skill developed by professional Muslim reciters. The Qur'an is regarded as the Word of God transmitted to Mohammed through the angel Gabriel

A young Turkish Muslim student illuminating a page from the Qur'an. (Courtesy of Turkish Tourism and Information Office)

from an original preserved in heaven. Thus, all of its one hundred and fourteen chapters, called *suras,* are believed to be eternal and uncreated.

It is not certain whether Mohammed could read or write, but almost from the start his followers took down what he recited, using scraps of parchment and leather, tablets of stone, ribs of palm branches: anything they could find to write on. Soon after their prophet's death, these fragments were collected and called the Qur'an.

The contents of the Qur'an are highly varied and suggest parallels with Judaism, Christianity and Zoroastrianism. Accounts from the Old Testament, the New Testament, and the Judaic traditions of the Mishnah and the Midrash, all have a place in the Qur'an. Some sections are purely Arabic in origin, and many passages deal with ceremonial and civil laws, though theological reflections and moral exhortations are included.

The arrangement of the Qur'an is arbitrary. With the exception of the first short sura, usually known as the "Lord's Prayer" of Islam and recited five times daily, the order of the suras seems to be determined by their length: the longest suras are placed first and the shorter ones toward the end. Here is the Muslim Lord's Prayer:

> In the name of Allah, the Merciful, the Compassionate!
>
> Praise be to Allah, the Lord of the worlds,
> The Merciful One, the Compassionate One,
> Master of the day of doom!
>
> Thee alone we serve, to Thee alone we cry for help!
> Guide us in the straight path,
> The path of them that Thou hast blessed,
> Not of those with whom Thou art angry,
> Nor of those who go astray.

The Qur'an, which has 114 chapters, is about the same length as the New Testament. Although non-Muslims refer to these chapters by numbers, Muslims identify them by names which are taken from some word or subject in the sura. For example, the second chapter is called "The Cow" and consists mainly of discussions about the Jews and their former worship of a "cow": possibly the golden calf of the Torah (Exodus 32). Many other chapters refer to Biblical characters such as Mary, Joseph, and Abraham. Adam is described as the first prophet, while Satan's fall from his position in Heaven among the angels is explained by his refusal to worship Adam on God's command. (The Qur'an refers to Satan as "Shaitan" or "Iblis" from the Greek word *diabolos,* meaning devil.) Moses is another prophet who is acknowledged as having "talked with God" and having given the Torah to the Jews. A number of other prophets are mentioned in the prophetic line culminating with Mohammed.

The Qur'an shows great reverence for Jesus. He is regarded not only as a Prophet, but also as Son of Mary, Servant of God, Word, and Messiah. Not only are the miracles of Jesus mentioned, but the Annunciation to Mary of the birth of Jesus, which resembles the account in St. Luke's Gospel, is recounted twice in the Qur'an. Moreover, there is a reference to the Last Supper and the Ascension. The Crucifixion appears to be denied, in that the Qur'an states, "they slew him not . . . but Allah raised him to Himself."

While the followers of Islam respect the Scriptures of Judaism and Christianity, they regard the Qur'an as the pure and final essence of divine revelation, superseding the other Scriptures. Its inspiration and authority are thought to extend to every letter and title (of which there are 323,621) so that every good Muslim must read the Qur'an in Arabic. Although the Qur'an has been translated into some forty languages, it is believed to lose much of its inspiration in translation; no translation has ever fully conveyed the eloquence or flavour of the original Arabic.

The Qur'an became the instrument for converting the whole Arab world from idol worship to belief in and devotion to the One and true God: Allah. Five central teachings stand out clearly in the Qur'an. They are defined as follows:

> True piety is this:
> To believe in Allah,
> And the Last Day,
> The Angels,
> The Book,
> And the Prophets . . .

Sura 2:176

GOD

The Muslim faith rests first of all on the basic conviction that there is but One God: Allah, which is a shortened form of *alillah,* meaning "The God". Much of the Qur'an's teaching about God is expressed in the form of adjectives, such as All-seeing, All-powerful, All-knowing, All-hearing, from which are derived the ninety-nine "beautiful names" of Allah. Occasionally, however, there are longer passages that attempt to describe the glory and power of Allah.

> Allah –
> There is no god but He,
> the Living, the Everlasting!
> Slumber seizes Him not, neither sleep;
> to Him belongs
> all that is in the heavens and the earth.
>
> Who is there that shall intercede with Him
> save by His leave?
> He knows what lies before them
> and what is after them,
> and they comprehend not anything of His knowledge
> save such as He wills.
>
> His Throne comprises the Heavens and the Earth;
> the preserving of them oppresses Him not;
> He is the All-high, the All-glorious!
>
> Sura 2:255-256

God exists from all eternity to all eternity. Everything comes into existence by his will and his creative word: "Be!" He commands, and it becomes. Allah is the only reality. He alone grants life and death. Men are his creatures and must submit their wills to his ways, no matter what he decrees! Although Allah is regarded as the Merciful, the Compassionate, the Loving, and the Forgiving towards penitents, he is also the Majestic, the Terrible, the Stern, who punishes all sinners.

Though Allah is "nearer to man than his neck-vein", yet at no time can he ever be within reach of man's knowledge and understanding. Man is called to believe, but in the end Allah is unknowable, except insofar as he chooses to reveal himself. He alone knows "the Unseen in the Heavens and the Earth" as well as "thoughts within the breasts" of men. He is the Creator, Protector and Provider of man and the universe.

> That then is Allah your Lord;
> there is no god but He,
> the Creator of everything!
> So serve Him,
> for He is Guardian over everything!
>
> Sura 6:102

Like Judaism then, Islam emphasizes the central doctrine of the Oneness of Allah. Mohammed accuses the Christians of being polytheists because of their belief in the Trinity. "Praise belongs to God," said he, "who has not taken to Him a son, and who has not any associate in the Kingdom" (Sura 17:110). God is One, and there is no other God except Allah.

THE LAST DAY

The Last Day, or the Day of Judgement, occupies a very important place in the Qur'an. The vivid descriptions of Heaven and Hell and the elaborate portrayal of the final judgement are very similar to the Book of Revelation in the New Testament and yet more powerful. The events of the Last Day are described as cataclysmic; that is, as appearing suddenly with great cosmic changes and at a time known only to God. On that Day, when the Trumpet sounds, the sun shall be darkened, the stars shall fall, the heavens shall be split asunder, the mountains shall turn to dust, and the earth shall be crushed.

> When the sun shall be darkened,
> When the stars shall be thrown down,
> When the mountains shall be set moving,
> When the pregnant camels shall be neglected,
> When the savage beasts shall be mustered,
> When the seas shall be set boiling . . .
> When the scrolls shall be unrolled,
> When the heavens shall be stripped off,
> When Hell shall be set blazing,
> When Paradise shall be brought nigh,
> Then shall a soul know what it has produced!
> When the Trumpet is blown with a single blast,
> And the earth and the mountains are lifted up
> and crushed with a single blow,
> Then, on That Day, the Terror shall come to pass . . .
> And the angels shall stand upon its borders . . .
> On That Day you shall be exposed,
> Not one secret of yours concealed.

Sura 81:1-14

On that Last Day, according to the Qur'an, the graves will open and men will be called to account. The guardian angel of each individual will bear witness to the man's record on earth. His deeds will be weighed in the divine Balance, and a Book will be placed in his hand.

If the Book is placed in his right hand, then he will be among the blessed; but if the Book is placed in his left hand, then he will be among the damned.

> Then as for him who is given his book in his *right* hand . . . he shall be in a pleasing life, in a lofty Garden . . .

> But as for him who is given his book in his *left* hand, he shall say, "Would that I had not been given my book and not known my reckoning! Would it had been the end!"
> Take him and fetter him, and then roast him in Hell!

Sura 69:13-37

No description can convey the terror of the Qur'anic portrayal of Hell. All worshippers of gods other than Allah, all the proud and the evil-doers, shall be cast into the fires of Hell. They will abide there forever, with no release from its torments. On the other hand, all the blessed and God-fearing individuals, all the humble and charitable, all those who suffered for Allah's sake, all those, especially, who fought in the name of, and for, Allah, shall be provided with fine garments, music, feasting, beautiful maidens and bliss no words can express in the Garden of Paradise.

Two important concepts emerge out of these descriptions. First, the picture of life after death depicted in the Qur'an justifies the notion of *al-jihad* ("the Holy War"), since death in battle fought on behalf of Allah guarantees a believer's entrance into Paradise. To put it differently, the Qur'an sanctions retaliation as a religious practice and supports it with powerful incentives:

> O believers, prescribed for you is retaliation . . .
> In retaliation there is life for you . . .
> Fight in the Way of God with those who fight with you,
> But aggress not; God loves not the aggressors.
> And slay them wherever you come upon them,
> And expel them from where they expelled you.
> Persecution is more grievous than slaying . . .
> Holy things demand retaliation.
> Whoso commits aggression against you,
> Do you commit aggression against him,
> Just as he has committed against you;
> And fear you Allah,
> And know that Allah is with the god-fearing!

Sura 2:172-196

The second concept is less well defined; it is the concept of free will. If Allah is All-powerful, All-present and All-knowing, then is everything pre-destined by him, or do men have a free will: can they make a choice? The Qur'an seems to sway between these two viewpoints. While Allah is regarded as the source of good and evil, and while Muslims are content to explain all events (whether joyful or disastrous) as the decree of Allah, yet the Qur'an often speaks of man's moral choice. Of course, all religions that predicate an Omnipotent (All-powerful), Omniscient (All-knowing) and Omnipresent (All-present) God, sooner or later have to face this dilemma. Suffice it to say that complete "submission" to the will of Allah is the controlling feature of Islam: "Allah has promised those of them who believe and do deeds of righteousness, forgiveness and a mighty wage."

THE ANGELS

The angels, as generally represented in the Qur'an, are Allah's messengers. Like men, they are Allah's creatures and servants who worship him continually. They record men's actions, receive their souls at death and witness for or against them on the Last Day. They guard the gates of Hell and support Allah's throne.

There are rebellious angels as well, who are called *jinn*. The jinn (also called *shaitans*), lead men astray, teach them sorcery, oppose the Prophets and try to overhear discussions and decisions in Heaven. They and their leader Shaitan or Iblis (Satan) share the same fate as men who, on the Last Day, are to be judged and condemned to Hell.

THE BOOK

Although the Qur'an refers to several anonymous scriptures, it accords special importance to the Books of Judaism and Christianity; it singles out three by name. According to the Qur'an, Moses was given the *Tawreh* (Arabic word for Torah); David received the *Zabur* (Psalms) and Jesus the *Injil* (Evangel or Gospel). These scriptures are regarded as revelations from Allah. But the final revelation, the Book of Books, containing the Perfect Truth, which Allah delivered through Mohammed, is the Qur'an.

Nowhere in the Qur'an (or for that matter in Islamic religion) is Mohammed described as divine. No miraculous powers are attributed to him. He is only a mortal man – a prophet – whose coming, according to the Qur'an, is foretold by Jesus. Again according to the Qur'an, Mohammed is mentioned by name in both the Tawreh and the Injil, though it is said that both Jews and Christians have concealed or possibly perverted the references to Mohammed.

The Qur'an also records the rules and regulations governing marriage, divorce, and personal and social relationships, all of which resemble the "pure" and "impure" regulations found in the book of Leviticus in the Torah. It also includes rules of prayer, the direction in which a worshipper must face in order to pray, fasting and prohibitions against eating pork, drinking wine, and playing games of chance. The Qur'an is unique among the sacred writings of the world in that it is the only collection attributed to one single human author.

THE PROPHETS

The importance of the doctrine of the Prophets is as great as the doctrine that proclaims the Oneness of Allah. To all peoples and in all ages, Allah sent "messengers" or prophets to proclaim the Oneness of God and to warn men of the future Judgement. The Qur'an mentions twenty-eight prophets in all, of whom Mohammed is the last, or "seal" of the prophets. Eighteen of these prophets are Old Testament figures, such as Adam, Noah, Abraham, Moses and David. Three are from the New Testament: Zechariah, John the Baptist and Jesus. Four are Arabian prophets, two are unknown, and the last is Mohammed himself. Just as all Muslims are required to believe in the Oneness of Allah, so are they required to believe in all these twenty-eight prophets.

The Qur'an relates further, that most of these prophets, if not all, were rejected and persecuted by their fellow countrymen. Some were endowed by God with special powers to perform miracles. Such was Jesus, who seems to hold a unique place among the prophets in Islam. He is said to have been born of the Virgin Mary, who was "chosen by God and purified above all women". Moreover, Jesus is regarded as the promised "Messiah, God's Word, God's Messenger, and the Spirit from God"

> People of the Book,
> Go not beyond the bounds in your religion . . .
> The Messiah, Jesus son of Mary,
> was only the Messenger of God,
> and His word that He committed to Mary,
> and a Spirit from Allah.
> So believe in Allah and His messengers,
> and say not, "Three".
> God is only One God!

Sura 4:171-172

Just as Adam is regarded by Muslims as the first prophet sent by Allah, so Mohammed is the last prophet by whom Allah reveals his eternal message in its definitive form.

The Five Pillars in Islam

Mohammed did not institute either an organized priesthood or any sacraments, but he did prescribe several practical religious duties. These observances are usually known as "The Five Pillars in Islam".

CREED – SHAHADAH

No religion in the world has a shorter or a more incisive creed than the Islamic profession of faith: *La ilaha illa'llah muhammadun rasulu'llah.* This means: "There is no other God but Allah (and) Mohammed is the Prophet of Allah." This brief, simple, and yet explicit sentence is the only creed pronounced. It is recited, not once a week in a formal service, but many times a day by countless devoted Muslims as they go about their work. Five times during the day, a similar, though somewhat longer formula, is proclaimed by the *muezzin*. A *muezzin* is one who calls people to prayer from the tower (minaret) of the Islamic mosque. The loud voice of a *muezzin* rather than pealing bells summons people to prayer:

> Allah is most Great! Allah is most Great!
> I bear witness that there is no god but Allah!
> I bear witness that Mohammed is the prophet of Allah!
> Come to prayer! Come to prayer!

PRAYER – SALAT

There is an Arabic parable that explains how each time a bird drinks a drop of water it lifts up its eyes in gratitude towards heaven. Similarly, a faithful Muslim shows his gratitude to Allah by praying five times a day: at daybreak, at noon, in mid-afternoon, after sunset, and before retiring to bed. Muslims are supposed to go to the mosque for prayer; but if that is not possible, then it does not matter where the religious duty is performed, as long as it is observed. Many men, therefore, pray at home or wherever they may happen to be. Women and girls pray, in general, at home, though they may go nowadays to the mosque, where a room or balcony is set aside for them.

First, preparation must be made by washing the head, hands, and feet with water. If no water is available, then hands and face may be wiped with fine, clean sand. Then a prayer mat is spread and the faithful kneels facing in the direction of Mecca. Because there is a fixed order of worship, the prayers and the sequence in which they occur are the same whether they are recited in a mosque or elsewhere. No matter what the language of the worshipper is, the prayers are recited in Arabic. Naturally, this schedule is not absolutely binding during times of sickness and travelling. In such circumstances the Qur'an recognizes the difficulties and hence prescribes a more relaxed ritual.

One day a week is set aside as a day of public prayer. What Saturday is for Judaism and Sunday for Christianity, Friday is for Islam. Every Friday noon, all Muslims join together in the mosque and its surrounding area for communal prayer. There are no images of any kind in the mosque, no paintings or pictorial windows, for Muslims dislike such representations. Instead, many Qur'anic texts are written on the walls in Arabic. There are no seats or pews in the mosque, since everyone must spread his carpet for prayer. Qur'anic texts are chanted and the service lasts half an hour.

Washing the head, hands, and feet is part of the preparation for prayer, and the courtyards of mosques are equipped with washing facilities. (Courtesy of Robert Monroe)

Muslims pray wherever they happen to be: at home, in the market, at a railway station, on board a ship, or by the roadside. Every Muslim unrolls his prayer mat and stands barefoot facing towards Mecca. Various formal positions are assumed during prayer: standing, bowing, kneeling, and prostrating by touching the ground with the forehead. (Courtesy of Robert Monroe)

ALMSGIVING — ZAKAT

Together with prayer the Qur'an stresses the giving of alms as the outward sign of true piety. In the early years of the Islamic religion, almsgiving was a free-will offering, but what began as a voluntary act of charity soon evolved into an obligatory tax, the *zakat*. The money collected in this way was used for the care of the poor, the building and support of mosques, and at one time during the great Islamic empire, for expenses incurred in the administration of the Islamic empire. With the disruption of the empire, the *zakat* has become a voluntary gift once more. Many devout Muslims regard it as a "loan" made to God, which he will repay many-fold.

FASTING

The most carefully observed of all Muslim religious duties is to fast during the month of Ramadan, the ninth month in the Muslim calendar, the month in which Mohammed is supposed to have received his first revelations. In order to commemorate this occasion, the faithful

are commanded to fast (without anything to eat or drink) from dawn till sunset for this whole month. However, since it is a month in a lunar calendar, Ramadan rotates around the year. When Ramadan falls in the winter months, a religious fast does not seem too demanding, but during the summer months, and in hot countries especially, this duty becomes particularly rigorous.

> O believers, prescribed for you is the Fast, even as it was prescribed for those that were before you . . .
> The month of Ramadan, wherein the Qur'an was sent down to be a guidance to the people, and as clear signs of the Guidance and the Salvation. So let those of you, who are present at the month, fast it; and if any of you be sick, or if he be on a journey, then a number of other days; God desires ease for you, and desires not hardship for you.

> Sura 2:183-185

PILGRIMAGE – HAJJ

Long before the days of Mohammed, Mecca had been a sacred centre to which Arabian people came yearly, on a pilgrimage to the sacred cube-shaped shrine known as the Ka'aba. In the shrine was a Black Stone about the size of a pomegranate and oval in shape. It was traditionally believed to have been brought down to Abraham by the angel Gabriel. Moreover, legend said that the holy Stone had once been so brilliantly white that pilgrims could be guided to the city by its radiance. Because of man's wickedness the stone had turned black.

Only a few steps away from the Ka'aba was the sacred well of Zam-zam, believed to contain miraculous healing powers, though later tradition connected it with Hagar, who, when she left Abraham's tent, wandered with her son Ishmael through the barren desert in search of water. In desperation, she left Ishmael, who was too exhausted to travel any further, lying on the hot earth, while she ran back and forth in search of water. In the meantime, Ishmael, tossing restlessly, kicked his heels and accidentally uncovered the opening to the well. Hagar and her son decided to remain there, and in the years to come the children and grandchildren of Ishmael multiplied to become the Arab race. (Arabs consider themselves sons of Abraham through Ishmael.)

The Black Stone in the Ka'aba and the well of Zamzam are not the only factors that made Mecca a holy city. Eight years after Mohammed had fled from Mecca to Medina, a delegation from Mecca negotiated a peaceful settlement with Mohammed. In January A.D. 630 Mohammed and some 10,000 followers peacefully entered Mecca, the city of his birth. Walking first seven times around the outside of the Ka'aba, Mohammed entered the shrine and destroyed all the 360 idols and images. Then he dedicated the Ka'aba to Allah and proclaimed Mecca to be the holiest city of Islam.

Each year following this incident, Mohammed came to Mecca from Medina to lead a large group of people in a pilgrimage to the holy Ka'aba. His last pilgrimage was in A.D. 632, when it is said that 100,000 faithful followers walked and performed many solemn rites. The pilgrimage (Hajj) to the Holy City then became a popular means of securing Allah's favour.

No religious ritual has done more to unite the Muslims than the rite of pilgrimage. Every true Muslim must make a pilgrimage to the sacred city of Mecca at least once in his lifetime. During the same period each year, hundreds of thousands of Muslims from all walks of life and of varying colour, race, and nationality (for example, Arabs, Turks, Persians, Negroes, Indians, Chinese) meet on common ground and realize their equality before Allah. Before entering the holy precincts, all pilgrims wear a white seamless garment and abstain from shaving or cutting their hair. However, simply visiting Mecca is not enough. Three main rituals and various other duties are prescribed:

1. Before entering the most sacred precincts of the very large open-air centre where the Ka'aba is located, pilgrims stop to perform their

ablutions, put on the white seamless garment, remove their sandals or shoes, and approach the Ka'aba barefoot. Then, like their prophet Mohammed, they walk around it seven times; three times quickly and four times slowly. On each circuit they pause to kiss – or if the crowd is too great – they pause to touch with the hand or a stick the southeast corner of the Ka'aba, where the Black Stone is located.

2. The next observance commemorates Hagar's frantic search for water for her son Ishmael. Pilgrims walk quickly seven times across the valley between the two mounds of Safa and Marwa, some five hundred yards apart.

3. The climactic ritual is a march to the Mount of Mercy, in the plain of Arafat, some fifteen miles east of Mecca. This ceremony is a day's journey on foot but many stop to rest at the sanctuary of Mina, the half-way point. All pilgrims must, however, arrive at Mount Mercy on the following morning. Once there, pilgrims "stand before Allah" from noon to sunset, absorbed in pious meditation. The night is then spent in the open. The following morning, pilgrims return to Mina, where animal sacrifices and three days of feasting follow. A final round of the Ka'aba in Mecca, and the discarding of the seamless garment completes the pilgrimage. The pilgrim is now permitted to assume the special title of *Hajj* – one who has made the pilgrimage to the Holy City.

Naturally, there are millions of Muslims for whom the pilgrimage is impossible; they either live too far from Mecca or cannot afford the expense of even a short journey. In such cases, the custom now is for the would-be pilgrim to contribute as much as he can afford so that a substitute can go in his place. The substitute brings merit upon all those who make his pilgrimage possible.

The Hadith

Next to the Qur'an, the most important Islamic text is the Hadith. The Hadith (Tradition) is a collection of the actions and sayings of the Prophet Mohammed. Naturally, the Prophet through whom the Qur-'an was revealed was considered the most competent and most appropriate authority to interpret it. Since his judgements were accepted at all times, his actions and sayings were regarded as "commentaries" to the Qur'an. But Mohammed never recorded them, so it was left to a human chain of reliable narrators to pass on the record in the form of the Hadiths. As one might suppose, there are a vast number of versions or editions of the Hadith, but no single collection has won the full acceptance of all Muslims. Certain compilers are trusted more than others, but what has been accepted by one school or sect has been rejected by another. One of the main reasons for this disagreement is that each version of the Hadith is a unique collection of events and sayings transmitted with the authority of a particular chain of narrators. To be acceptable, the Hadith must include the name of each human link in the chain between the Prophet and the man who recorded the Prophet's life and words. Here, for example, is the opening statement of a typical Hadith:

> Al-Bukhari writes: "Abdallah ibn-al-Aswad told me: Al-Fadl ibn-al-Ata told us: Isma'il ibn-Umayya told us on the authority of Yahya ibn-Abdallah ibn-Sayfi that he heard Abu Ma'bad, the freedman of Ibn-Abbas, say, 'I heard Ibn-Abbas say:' 'When the Prophet,' the blessings of Allah be upon him, and peace, 'sent Mu'adh to the Yemen, he said to him . . . ' "

The question that obviously bothers the scholar is: what faith can he place on the authority or reliability of each transmitter? To be sure, many Muslim scholars admit that many Hadiths are spurious, but no way has yet been devised to check out or confirm the authenticity of the names mentioned in the chain or of the tradition transmitted by a particular version of the Hadith. Nevertheless, a great deal of precious information, which would otherwise have gone unrecorded, is preserved in the Hadith; for example, the moral precepts of the Prophet. True, the general principles by which all moral issues must be regulated are in the Qur'an, but not all the issues are clearly elaborated there. In addition, almost all of the early history of Islam and the religious opinions of the first generations of pious Muslims can be deduced from various versions of the Hadith. Therefore, even though the authenticity of certain versions of the Hadith may be questioned, their historical and moral value should not be underestimated.

The Spread of Islam

Unlike most religions, which grew slowly from remote beginnings, Islam took shape within the lifetime of Mohammed and spread with the speed and violence of a hurricane. For a quarter of a century after Mohammed's death, the leadership was continued successively by four Caliphs (successors): Abu Bakr, Omar, Othman and Ali. Under their skilled leadership Islam in less than thirty years overran Egypt, Palestine, Syria, Iraq and the Persian Empire. All these nations fell to the Islamic wave between the years A.D. 635 – 651.

Shortly after the establishment of this vast empire, Islam was plunged into civil war on the question of the Caliphate (succession). Ali's leadership was contested by Mu'awiyah, the Governor of Syria. Eventually Ali was murdered by an assassin's dagger, and thereafter permanent political divisions arose.

THE UMMAYAD DYNASTY (A.D. 661 – 750)

The Ummayad Caliphs moved their capital from Medina to Damascus, and under their capable rule the Muslim empire reached its greatest expansion. The momentum of conquest carried them eastwards to India as far as the borders of China, and westward to the Atlantic, across the Straits of Gibraltar into Spain, Portugal, and France. At last in A.D. 733 (one hundred years after the Prophet's death) the Muslims were halted at Tours by the Franks. Because of this decisive battle, Europe remained Christian.

Mosques can be erected on large grounds or squeezed between commercial buildings, as here. This is the Daratagaha mosque in Colombo, Ceylon. (Courtesy of BOAC)

THE ABBASSID DYNASTY (A.D. 750 – 1258)

Although intermittently other Caliphs tried to disrupt the Ummayad Dynasty, it was not until A.D. 750, some seventeen years after the battle of Tours, that the Ummayads were overthrown by a new Arabian dynasty which represented the interests of the Islamized Persian aristocracy. Hence, shortly after his victory, the new Caliph moved his capital from Damascus to Baghdad, deep within the old Persian empire, and close to the ruins of ancient Babylon. Six years later a rival Caliphate was temporarily established by the Ummayads in Cordova, Spain (A.D. 756 – 1031).

The Abbassid Dynasty enjoyed the longest reign of any in Islam (over 530 years) though its influence declined after the middle of the ninth century A.D., when political power shifted to independent local dynasties. However, under the early Abbassids, Baghdad became one of the world's leading cities and the centre of a vast commercial network spreading across and far beyond the Muslim empire. The splendour of this great city and the Caliphs who ruled there have become familiar to us through the tales of the *Arabian Nights*.

Exposed for some time to the Greco-Roman, Byzantine, Persian, and Indian heritages, Islam evolved a brilliant culture of its own. The wealth and culture of Baghdad reached its zenith under the reign of Harun-al-Rashid (A.D. 736 – 809) which is regarded as the "Golden Age" of Islam. Science and the fine arts flourished. Mathematics and medicine advanced in a period when Europe was relatively backward. Muslim architects created masterpieces like the mosque of Cordova in Spain (now a Christian cathedral). Philosophy and poetry flourished throughout the Muslim Empire.

At a time when Charlemagne, the Christian Emperor of the western kingdoms, was struggling desperately to civilize his semi-barbaric Franks, Harun-al-Rashid reigned over glittering Baghdad, and collected taxes from the non-Islamic nations in his empire. Even the Byzantine Empire (representing the Eastern Christian Orthodox Church) paid tribute to Harun-al-Rashid. When on one occasion the tribute was discontinued, Harun-al-Rashid sent the following note:

> In the name of Allah, the Merciful, the Compassionate.
> From Harun, the commander of the Faithful,
> To Nicephorus, the dog of a Roman.
> Verily I have read your letter, O son of an infidel mother!
> As for the answer, it shall be for your eye to see, not for your ear to hear! Salam!

This letter was followed by a successful military coup which forced the Byzantine Empire to resume its tribute.

Late in the ninth century A.D., the great Muslim Empire slowly began to disintegrate, as several independent dynasties sprang up. Eastern Persia (Iran), Syria, and Egypt broke free of Abbassid control and established their own Caliphates. But by this time the Abbassid Dynasty was slowly losing its grip on its own government in Baghdad. The final blow came in A.D. 1258 when Baghdad was sacked by the Mongols, an Asiatic group of people. Half a century later the Mongols embraced Islam and made it the state religion, while Babur, a later descendant, founded the great Muslim Empire in India.

THE OTTOMAN DYNASTY (1295 – 1924)

It was not the Mongols who restored Islam's military glory, but the Ottoman Turks, who were the last Muslim Dynasty to hold the Caliphate. Making Constantinople (Istanbul) the capital of Islam, the Ottoman Turks nominally united most of the Near and Middle East under their rule, though they had to recognize the independence of Persia in the East and of Morocco in the West. They continued to control diminishing territories until 1924, when the Turkish Republic replaced the autocratic rule of the Ottoman Caliphate.

The Sultan Ahmet Mosque in Turkey (also called the Blue Mosque) was built in the early seventeenth century as an imperial mosque and included a theological school, library, and hospice for the poor. It is the world's only mosque with six minarets (towers) and stands on the site of the ancient Hippodrome, which was used for horse and chariot races in Roman times. (Courtesy of Robert Monroe)

The interior of the Sultan Ahmet Mosque is especially noted for the beauty of the blue tiles that cover the interior walls and for the nearly three hundred windows from which the reflection of light gives the building a mystic air. There are no images of any kind, no paintings or pictorial windows, since Muslims consider man to be created in the image of God and believe that any representation of the human form is an insult to God. (Courtesy of Turkish Tourism and Information Office)

Islamic Sects

Islam has not escaped a fate common to all religions: sectarian divisions. Although Islam originated in Arabia and its message was largely a reflection of the unique character and personality of the Arabian people, its rapid spread outside Arabia brought within its fold widely differing peoples. This gave rise to serious differences in teachings and interpretations.

Although there are sub-sects, the two main branches of Islam are the Sunni and the Shi'ite. They split over the question of the line of succession from Mohammed. The Sunni, the major and the orthodox branch of Islam, recognize the first four Caliphs as true successors of Mohammed. The Shi'ite, a minority group which represents the liberal branch of Islam and is mainly concentrated in Iran and India, disregard the first three Caliphs who were not related to Mohammed, uphold family succession only and regard Ali (son-in-law of Mohammed) and his successors as divinely ordained Caliphs.

A Shi'ite sub-group, known as the "Twelvers", recognizes twelve Imams (religious leaders) since the death of the Prophet Mohammed. The members of this sect believe that there is yet one more Imam to come who may appear at any time to conquer the world and usher in justice and righteousness.

In 1844, in Shirez, Persia, twenty-five-year-old Ali Mohammed proclaimed himself to be yet another Imam, and promised that one greater than himself would follow him and complete his work of reform. Although he attracted a large following, his views excited the hostility of both the political and religious establishment of Persia, and he was executed in 1850. Two years later, a follower of Ali Mohammed attempted to assassinate the Shah of Persia. A widespread persecution of this new group followed. Among those who were banished to Baghdad there was one, Mirza Husein Ali, who was the son of a government official. In 1863, he proclaimed himself to be the Messiah of whom Ali Mohammed had spoken. He assumed a new name, Baha Ullah (Glory of God), and those who accepted his leadership came to be called Bahais.

Although five years later, in 1868, Baha Ullah was interned by the Ottoman Government for thirty years, he continued to inspire and organize adherents to the new faith through extensive correspondence until his death in 1898. Through the efforts of his followers the movement spread beyond the borders of countries usually associated with belief in Islam. Baha Ullah considered that great religious figures in the world were the recipients of divine revelation: Moses, Zoroaster, Jesus, the Buddha, Krishna, and, of course, Mohammed. Moreover, he instigated social and religious reform. He rejected polygamy, slavery, and the concept of the *jihad* (holy war). He strongly favoured raising the status of women. Ritual practices were simplified. Pursuit of virtue, devotional meditation, and prayer became, under his leadership, the core of religious activity. Belief in angels and demons was dropped, while the concept of heaven and hell was treated symbolically.

The faith of Bahaism continued to spread beyond the Islamic world. With its vision of a world-wide community under one federal, world government, speaking a single world language as a means of promoting human unity, Bahaism attracts rational and pious men of all nations. Naturally, in its efforts to achieve the union of all men, it has gone beyond the Islamic creed which states: "There is no other God but Allah and Mohammed is the Prophet of Allah!" Whether Bahaism can now be regarded as an offshoot of Islam or as a new religion lying outside the stream of Islam is an interesting question for personal speculation.

There are various other sub-groups of Islam, each of which reflects differences in points of doctrine and ritual practices. One of the most notable schools is the mystic group known as the Sufi, a word derived from the Arabic term *suf,* meaning "undyed wool". A Sufi, then, is one

who wears undyed wool because of its simplicity. Originally the movement was concerned with self-discipline, but later it changed its emphasis to the attainment of inner illumination and, especially, union
with Allah. Sufism, as Muslim mysticism is generally known, represents
an aspect of Islam that has appeared widely in various religious cultures under various names.

In the latter half of the nineteenth century, a new group called the
Ahmadiya arose in India. Both North Americans and Europeans have
come into contact with this group, which tends to re-interpret the
teachings of Islam in order to appeal to westerners.

The abolition of the Ottoman Caliphate in 1924 and Turkey's sub-
stitution of European political and social codes for Qur'anic law may
have dealt the religion of Islam its most serious blow. Nevertheless
many Islamic scholars are attempting to work out a re-interpretation
of Islam that fits the modern, secular world, and to maintain the rite
of pilgrimage as a means to preserve the sense of world solidarity
among its followers, a powerful feature of Islam.

HINDUISM

OM:
Mystical symbol of Hinduism

They call It Indra, Mitra, Varuna and Agni
And also Heavenly, Beautiful Garutman:
The Real is One, though sages name It variously . . .

Rig Veda I, 164.46

HINDUISM

One of the oldest surviving religions in the world, with an unbroken succession of seers and teachers, is practised by millions of people living in the vast subcontinent of India; it is known as Hinduism. The term "Hinduism" was coined in relatively recent times. Modern Hindus use this Western term simply as a convenience when speaking or writing in English. Among themselves they prefer to call their religion *sanatana dharma* ("eternal religion"), since it was not founded by any historical person but is based upon eternal principles that were "heard" by the *rishis* (sages or seers) who lived during a very remote period in history.

India is an ancient land and the Indians themselves are a mixed group of people. Before 2500 B.C. various tribes lived in India, including a curly-haired and black-skinned people known as the Dravidians. Some time in the middle of the second millenium B.C. a group of tribes known as the Aryans (meaning "Noble People") invaded India from the northwest and established themselves first on the northern branches of the Indus river and later in central and south India. The Aryans were tall and light-skinned and spoke an Indo-European language from which Sanskrit developed. Their culture and religion was related to that of the ancient Greeks, Romans, and Iranians.

Unfortunately, very little is known of pre-Aryan culture and religion. Archaeological excavations around the Indus Valley started at the turn of the century, and though there is evidence that a complex civilization must have existed before the Aryan invasion, there is little possibility of penetrating the culture and tradition of the pre-Aryans. However, successive waves of Aryan invasions and clashes between the Aryans and the Dravidians gave rise to distinct social classes, from which the "castes" of later Hindu society arose. Furthermore, as the Aryans firmly settled in all parts of India, the impact of their religion upon the beliefs of the people they conquered produced an extensive oral tradition passed on from generation to generation in folk-tales and epic stories. At the same time, the hymns and prayers of the priests expressed numerous religious concepts. Eventually, many of the hymns, prayers, epics and traditions came to be considered as sacred writings.

Hindu Sacred Writings

Hinduism recognizes two categories of sacred writings: *sruti* and *smriti.* The first term means "hearing" and applies to a group of writings which are considered to be eternal sacred knowledge heard by the *rishis.* Writings known as the Vedas (also referred to as Samhitas or "collections"), the Brahmanas, the Aranyakas and the Upanishads all belong to this group and are collectively known as The Veda – literally meaning "knowledge" or "sacred knowledge". The second term, *smriti,* means "memory" and applies to another group of writings, which are considered to be the records remembered and transmitted from generation to generation. Writings known as the Epics, the Code of Manu, the Sutras, and the Puranas all belong to this group. Each group of sacred writings, *sruti* or *smriti,* serves distinct purposes and fulfils different needs.

THE VEDA

The first category of writings, known collectively as The Veda, is divisible into four groups.

The Vedas or Samhitas

This collection consists of four Vedas composed sometime between 1500 B.C. and 800 B.C., known as the Rig-Veda, the Sama-Veda, the Yajur-Veda and the Atharva-Veda.

The Rig-Veda is a collection of about one thousand hymns, mostly of prayer and praise, to either a single deity or to a group of deities.

The Sama-Veda consists mainly of rhythmic chants borrowed from the Rig-Veda. The Sama-Veda is unique in that its verses and the order in which they are arranged have a special significance in the *soma* sacrifice. Soma is a plant recently identified as the *amanita muscaria,* a kind of mushroom, the intoxicating juice of which the priests used for sacrificial rituals.

The Yajur-Veda contains, in addition to verses taken from the Rig-Veda, many original prose formulae dealing with sacrificial ritual.

Moreover, the Yajur-Veda exists in two versions commonly known as the White Yajur-Veda and the Black Yajur-Veda.

The Atharva-Veda consists of a special class of texts dealing with charms, magical spells, incantations, and kingly duties.

The Brahmanas

This is a large collection of supplements to the Samhitas, containing directions for the proper ritual use of the hymns and prayers. The Brahmanas also include a great deal of mythological material concerning the origin and development of the universe. Certain experts regard the Brahmanas as the textbooks of the different schools of Brahmins (priests), since they give practical instructions – in minute detail – for the performance and conduct of all kinds of sacrifices. Be that as it may, the Brahmanas are a voluminous body of writings describing in exhaustive detail ritual observances and sacrifices, and discussing the mystical meanings of various rites. Each of the four Vedas is supplemented by its own Brahmana or Brahmanas. The Rig-Veda has two Brahmanas: the Aitareya and the Kanshitaki. The White Yagur-Veda is supplemented by the famous Satapatha-Brahmana; the Black Yagur-Veda, by the Taittiriya-Brahmana. The Sama-Veda is supplemented by eight Brahmanas; the Atharva-Veda, by one. The suggested dates for the Brahmanas vary from 800 B.C. to 300 B.C.

The Aranyakas

These sacred writings represent a further collection of the Brahmanas, mainly for those who retire into the forest and are unable to perform ritual sacrifices. They are esoteric in content and are concerned with the inmost nature of man and the universe.

The Upanishads

The Upanishads are a large collection of writings attached to the end of the Aranyakas. The Upanishads are regarded as the basic philosophic framework of Hinduism: they constitute the "end of sacred knowledge" (Vedanta) and their importance can scarcely be exaggerated. They are a collection of speculative texts; they have no single authorship and they do not attempt to present a logical, coherent view of reality. Most scholars suggest that the Upanishads developed over a period of three to four centuries – perhaps from 800 B.C. to 500 B.C.

These four groups complete the first category of sacred writings – the *sruti*. The more important of the second category of writings (the *smriti*) are the following:

THE EPICS

There are two great Hindu epics known as the Mahabharata and the Ramayana. The Mahabharata is not only the longer of the two; it is the longest epic in the world. It is over seven times the combined length of the Greek classical epics of the *Iliad* and the *Odyssey,* and contains some 220,000 lines. As a matter of fact, it is not all strictly epic since more than half of it contains material dealing with politics, law, religion and other topics. Undoubtedly, it is the work of many authors and the entire work was probably completed by the second or third century A.D. There are within the Mahabharata three famous stories that are greatly loved by Hindus, of which the favourite is the Bhagavad Gita. It is written in the form of a dialogue between a warrior and the Blessed Lord Krishna, disguised as the warrior's charioteer, and it owes its popularity to its emphasis on the "Path of Devotion" as the way of salvation.

The shorter of the two great epics is the Ramayana. It recounts the story of a prince called Rama who is exiled to the forest for fourteen years because of a rival half-brother and the intrigues of a jealous mother. In the meantime, Sita, Rama's ever-faithful wife, is abducted by a wicked demon. Unable to find her, Rama is aided by his friend Hanuman, the monkey, who succeeds in restoring Sita to her husband. Rama, Sita and Hanuman have long since become deified and are objects of worship for millions of Hindus.

THE CODE OF MANU

Compiled sometime before the second century A.D., the Code of Manu is accepted by most branches of Hinduism as the most complete expression of Hindu sacred law. Manu is traditionally considered to be the father of mankind (somewhat like Adam) and the founder of social and moral order. The book includes marriage laws, dietary regulations, the duties of a rajah, civil and criminal laws, daily rites and sacrifices, as well as statements on a variety of ethical subjects. Although many practices and rules are no longer followed in detail in India, these laws still have enormous cultural influence on daily life.

THE PURANAS

The word *purana* means "ancient" and refers to a collection of ancient lore, mythological material on the genealogy of gods, sages, and kings, and writings on the creation, destruction and re-creation of the universe. The Puranas, eighteen of which are generally held to be authoritative, are considered to be the product of theistic developments during the first millenium A.D.

Early Indian Religion

Virtually all our knowledge of the early stages of Indian religion comes from the study of the Vedas. Numerous hymns and prayers indicate belief in various gods or deities. Some of the deities are familiar to us through their Greek and Roman counterparts: Dyaus Pithar (Father Sky) whom the Greeks called Zeus-Pater and the Romans called Jupiter. Others, such as Indra, Varuna, Agni, Mitra, were prominent deities to whom devotees chanted adoringly.

> O mighty Varuna, now and hereafter, even as of old, will we speak forth our worship.
> For in Thyself, invincible God, Thy statutes ne'er to be moved are fixed as on a mountain.

> Move far from me what sins I have committed; let me not suffer, King, for guilt of others.
> Full many a morn remains to dawn upon us: in these, O Varuna, while we live, direct us.
>
> Rig-Veda II, 28

Hindus from all over India gather at the Har-Ki-Pauri Temple in Hardwar, Uttar Pradesh, for religious celebration. Many take a holy bath in the waters of the Ganges. (Courtesy of Government of India Tourist Office, Toronto)

Expressions that seem so primitive and simple should not prevent us from recognizing in them concerns which are still echoed by modern man. These concerns result from man's inner conflicts, of his awareness of the vast, mysterious universe, and of his search for an Ultimate Reality that gives meaning to his existence. Moreover, man's attempt to explain or describe his religious experiences – his attempt to put them into words – is not restricted to particular geographical, social, cultural, or religious circumstances. At different times, in different places, and in different socio-cultural environments, man has experienced the presence of the Absolute, of the Infinite, and suddenly realized how utterly limited and finite he was.

Whether man is a monotheist and believes in only one god or a polytheist and believes in many, he reaches out to express his deep admiration, love and devotion, to One who is mighty and worthy of his praises:

> I will declare the manly deeds of Indra, the first that he achieved, the thunder-wielder. He slew the dragon, then disclosed the waters and cleft the channels of the mountain torrents.
>
> Rig-Veda I, 32

Just as others pray to God for guidance and blessing in matters of daily life – be they personal, family, or business matters – so did the Hindus pray for help with their own daily problems, and their prayers took the form of casting spells:

A Prayer for Success in Gambling

> The successful, victorious, skilfully gaming Apsara [female Divinity], that Apsara who makes the winnings in the game of dice, do I call hither.
>
> The skilfully gaming Apsara who sweeps and heaps up the stakes, that Apsara who takes the winnings in the game of dice, do I call hither.
>
> May she [Apsara], who dances about with the dice, when she takes the stakes from the game of dice, when she desires to win for us, obtain the advantage of her magic!
>
> Atharva-Veda IV, 38

A Prayer to Arouse Passionate Love

May love, the disquieter, disquiet thee;
do not hold out upon thy bed!
With the terrible arrow of Kama [god of love]
do I pierce thee in the heart!

The arrow, winged with longing, barbed with love,
whose shaft is undeviating desire,
with that, well aimed,
Kama shall pierce thee in the heart!

Consumed by burning ardour, with parched mouth,
do thou, woman, come to me,
thy pride laid aside, mine alone,
speaking sweetly and to me devoted!

I drive thee with a goad from thy mother
and thy father,
so that thou shalt be in my power,
shalt come up to my wish!

All her thoughts do ye, O Mitra and Varuna,
drive out of her!
Then, having deprived her of her will,
put her into my power alone!

Atharva-Veda III, 25

The religion practised in the Vedic age (the early period of the Vedas) should by no means be regarded as simple or primitive. A complex system of rituals and sacrifices were performed by a special class of priests. These priests prepared the materials for sacrifice, recited the appropriate words, and performed the correct ritual. The sacrifice consisted of various offerings: the flesh of an animal, grain, vegetables, and milk. A combination of these offerings were in part poured or cast into the fire, in part placed on the ground on cushions of grass, and in part consumed by the participants in the sacrifice. Invoking the gods, the priests recited the following ritual:

Thou hast made prayers the means of Thine exalting.
We therefore wait on Thee with hymns O Indra . . .

Be delighted; note our sacrificial cake, Indra; drink soma
and the milk . . .
Be seated here on the sacrificer's grass.

Rig-Veda VI.23.6,7

These sacrifices seem to have served three purposes; first, as gifts
to the deities from whom gifts (such as long life, many children, health,
wealth, victory in fighting, and all the blessings one can enjoy in this
world) were expected in return; second, as offerings to remove guilt
("sin offerings") incurred either by contact with forbidden (taboo)
objects, or by any misdeeds, or by incorrect performance of rituals;
and, third, as a communal meal shared with the deities in which the
virtues of the deities passed to the faithful devotee through the sacrificial parts consumed by him.

So significant an event in itself was the sacrifice, that eventually it
came to be regarded as a cosmic, sacramental ritual. Indeed, the universe was held to have originated in a cosmic, human sacrifice. Thus,
the original cosmic Man, called Purusha, produced gods from himself
who made a sacrifice of him (Purusha):

The Purusha has a thousand heads, a thousand eyes, and a
thousand feet.
Encompassing the world on every side, He exceeded it by
ten fingers' length.
Purusha alone is all this universe, what has been, and what
is yet to be . . .
All creatures are one-fourth of Him; three-quarters are the
immortal in heaven . . .
When the gods performed the sacrifice with Purusha, spring
was the melted butter, summer the fuel, and autumn the obla-
tion. The gods, the celestial beings, and the seers performed
the sacrifice with Him . . .

Rig-Veda X.90

The basic identity is clear: the universe and everything in it, as well
as all celestial beings, *is* Purusha. Creation, therefore, is a sacrifice.
Henceforth, the sacrificial ritual performed by the priests was regarded
as a creative act.

Before long, certain profound thinkers began to question various
traditional views and religious values. By questioning and doubting,
they were simply displaying positive characteristics inherent in human
nature. For instance, if no one had questioned the traditional view of

the world, we would all still believe that the world is flat. But because one man doubted such a traditional view and persisted in proving the validity of his doubt, he was responsible for a tremendous change in the human concept of the earth and all the consequences of such a dynamic change. There are many other examples of progress as the direct result of doubt, but this is not the place to list them. It is enough to say that many phenomena once explained by reference to spirits both good and evil, to superstition and to magical power yielded new and more satisfying interpretations as a result of doubt. Because religious leaders like Buddha and Jesus doubted the validity of traditional views, they broke through into new religious dimensions and influenced the lives of millions.

One Indian mind questioned the nature of the universe and the role of the gods towards man and the universe. This man was not content with the religious answers of his age. "Why can there not be one cosmic principle, instead of many, that underlies everything?" he must have thought to himself. "Who brought everything into being and how? Who, or what, was before the gods?" The attention of this profound sage centred more and more upon the mysterious First Principle, the First Cause, the Essence, the Absolute. His inquiry led him to explain the universe as evolving out of That One – *tad ekam* – which was absolutely uncharacterizable, indescribable, without qualities or attributes. Furthermore, That One was neither existent nor non-existent but beyond being and non-being:

> Then was not non-existent nor existent:
> there was no realm of air, no sky beyond it.
> What covered in, and where and what gave shelter?
> Was water there, unfathomed depth of water?
>
> Death was not then, nor was there aught immortal:
> no sign was there, the day's and night's divider.
> That One breathed without breath by its own nature;
> apart from it was nothing else whatsoever.
>
> Darkness there was; at first hidden by darkness,
> this All was indiscriminated chaos.
> All that existed then was void and formless:
> by the great power of warmth That One was born.
>
> Who truly knows and who can here declare it,
> whence it was born and whence came this creation?

> The gods are later than this world's production.
> Who knows, then, whence it first came into being?
>
> He, the first origin of this creation,
> whether he formed it all or did not form it,
> Whose eye controls this world in highest heaven,
> he verily knows it, or perhaps he knows not.
>
> Rig-Veda X, 129

There is a close parallel between this remarkable statement and the Hebraic concept of creation in Genesis:

> The earth was without form and void,
> and darkness was upon the face of the deep . . .
>
> Genesis 1:2

Before anything existed or non-existed, before there was any realm of air or sky, before there was any death or deathlessness, and before light or darkness, day or night, there was That One. When man is in search of an Ultimate Reality, time, place and circumstances have no significance except to force him to express his discovery in terms of the culture of his environment.

The Rise of the Caste System

By the close of the seventh century B.C. there were in India a number of distinct organized principalities ruled like kingdoms by hereditary rajahs. Four distinct social groups began a subtle evolution. The priests had developed great power. In fact, a power struggle for social prestige ensued between the ruling rajahs and the priests. The ruling nobles, who were constantly fighting and gaining new territory, had to rely upon the priests to perform the necessary religious functions. The priests claimed that through their supernatural powers they could control and change the very course of cosmic events by the use of rituals and sacrifices.

While their rulers were campaigning, the priests were gaining popular esteem in the huts of the ordinary people. These priests claimed that if sacrifices, ceremonies, and rituals were performed properly in the prescribed manner of the Brahmanas (treatises compiled by the priests) they, the priests, could procure the desired results. Within the next few hundred years (by about 500 B.C.) the caste system gradually established itself and in its final form, according to the priests, consisted of four distinct groups:

BRAHMINS (priests). Occupying the central place of power within Hindu society are the Brahmins. With a deep passion to appreciate the values that matter most in human life, the Brahmins function as the spiritual and intellectual leaders of their society.

KSHATRIYAS (warriors). Chieftains, rulers, nobles and military protectors comprise the second caste, whose organizational function is to administer and promote the material welfare of society.

VAISYAS (craftsmen). All artisans, tradesmen, merchants and farmers who contribute to the economic well-being of the society rank next.

SUDRAS (labourers). At the bottom of the scale are those who supply the manual labour, including at one time, the slaves. From the sudras a fifth category gradually developed whose status is so low that they belong to no caste at all and are referred to as the "outcasts" or "untouchables".

The Hindu caste system cannot be regarded simply as a social scale of class distinction. Linked with the social manifestation is a religious justification known as *karma-samsara:* each man's birth into a particular caste is determined by the actions of his previous existence or existences. This religious law is explained more fully later; the point to be made here is that each caste defines a man's social and religious status, as well as his duties and obligations.

The Upanishadic Philosophy

Along with the development of ritual and sacrifice, philosophical and mystical speculation arose. Opinions regarding one cosmic principle were being formulated by many alert minds. Various writings seem to reflect a growing sense of a "principle of unity" in the universe. Could there be one Ultimate Reality that pervades the whole world? Who is man and what is his relationship to the Ultimate? Such philosophical questions were destined to be answered in the Upanishads.

It is impossible in a brief review like this to analyse all the speculative writings recorded in the Upanishads. What follows is an examination of certain basic views, especially in regard to the nature of the universe, the Ultimate Reality, and the purpose of man's existence in this world.

BRAHMAN-ATMAN

One of the striking features of the Upanishads is the recognition of Absolute Reality: that which transcends time, space and causality, and cannot be comprehended by human thought; that which pervades the universe and yet remains beyond it; that which is never seen but is all-seeing, which is never heard but is the hearer. This Absolute Reality is called Brahman.

The disciple asked: Om! By whose will directed does the mind proceed to its object? . . .

The teacher replied: It is the Ear of the ear, the Mind of the mind, the Speech of the speech, the Life of life, and the Eye of the eye . . .

The eye does not go thither, nor speech, nor the mind . . .

That which cannot be expressed by speech, but by which speech is expressed . . .

That which cannot be apprehended by the mind, but by which, they say, the mind is apprehended . . .

That which cannot be perceived by the eye, but by which the eye is perceived . . .

That which cannot be heard by the ear, but by which the hearing is perceived . . .

That which cannot be smelt by the breath, but by which the breath smells an object . . .

That alone know as Brahman, and not that which people here worship.

Kena Upanishad I, 1-9

The Upanishads describe Brahman sometimes as a personal being endowed with qualities and sometimes as an impersonal being devoid of any qualifying characteristics. Moreover, Brahman is all that is objective as well as subjective. In other words, Brahman is the whole, external world that exists outside of us as well as the whole inner being, self, or soul of each one of us. The Sanskrit word *atman* denotes the innermost and unseen self of an individual, which also includes his feeling, will-power and self-consciousness. All that goes on in one's whole inward world is a manifestation, a representation of That One: Brahman. That is to say, contrary to man's notion of the individuality of a human being, Hinduism insists on the absolute identity between the Universal Self (Brahman) and the individual self (atman). And this is true of every atman, be it in man, beast, bird, fish or vegetable. "Explain this to me," an inquirer cries eagerly, "who is Brahman?" "He is your Self!" comes the answer.

He who inhabits the earth, yet is within the earth, whom the earth does not know, whose body the earth is, and who controls the earth from within – He is your Self, the Inner Controller, the Immortal.

He who inhabits water, yet is within water, whom water does not know, whose body water is, and who controls water from within – He is your Self, the Inner Controller, the Immortal.

He who inhabits fire, yet is within fire . . .

He who inhabits the sky, yet is within the sky . . .

He who inhabits the air, yet is within the air . . .

He who inhabits heaven, yet is within heaven . . .

He who inhabits the sun, yet is within the sun . . .

He who inhabits all beings, yet is within all beings, whom no beings know, whose body all beings are, and who controls all beings from within – He is your Self, the Inner Controller, the Immortal.

Brihadaranyaka Upanishad III.7.3-23

The most significant contribution of the Upanishads to the Hindu religion is this idea of the utter oneness of *Brahman-atman*. The identification of the individual "self" with the universal "Self" in a mystical experience establishes the existence of a Reality which is infinite, unlimited, directly perceived and spiritual. Neither philosophical speculation nor any kind of reasoning can penetrate deeper than this metaphysical reality: the non-duality of existence. Hence, Hindus do not believe that man is "created in the image of God" but that "man is God"; he is divine. The universe and everything in the universe, including man, is not to be considered as something apart and distinct from the Absolute Being; it *is* the Absolute Being! There is no subject-object, no "I" and no "you". The Absolute is not "up there" or "beyond" but within. The First Principle of things must not be sought in the external but in man's inmost self. Thus, the true "self" of man and the Ultimate Universal "Self" are one; they are identical. This identity is most emphatically expressed in a famous formulae: *tat tvam asi*, which means, "That art thou!"

This notion, that the Divine Being pervades the whole world, is illustrated by a number of parables, summed up in the Upanishads in the story of Uddalaka and his son.

"As bees, my dear," explains the father to his son, "make honey by collecting the juices of trees located at different places, and reduce them to one form; and as these juices have no discrimination (so as to be able to say): 'I am the juice of this tree,' or 'I am the juice of that tree' – even so, indeed, my dear, all these creatures, though they reach Pure Being, do not know they have reached Pure Being. . . . Now that which is the subtle essence – in it all that exists has its self. That is the True. That is the Self. That thou art."

Chandogya Upanishad VI.9.1-2

In other words, just as the nectar of different flowers is transformed into honey, so is the individual transformed, losing his identity in a higher reality. Nevertheless, there could be no honey without nectar and there can be no state of Pure Being without individuals.

Such a simple but profound analogy is not too satisfactory to the son and so he inquires further into the meaning of "That thou art!"

> "Please, venerable Sir, give me further instruction," says the son.
> "So be it, my dear," Uddalaka replies. "These rivers, my dear, flow – the eastern towards the east, and the western towards the west. They arise from the sea and flow into the sea. Just as these rivers, while they are in the sea, do not know: 'I am this river' or 'I am that river', even so, my dear, all these creatures even though they have come from Pure Being, do not know that they have come from Pure Being. . . . Now, that which is subtle essence – in it all that exists has its self. That is the True. That is the Self. That thou art."
> Chandogya Upanishad VI.10.1-3

This second illustration is designed to help the son see that the individual self and the Absolute Universal Self are one. Just as the individual rivers originate from the sea (the winds pick up moisture and return it to the land as precipitation) and flow back into the sea, thus becoming identical with the sea by merging in the greater whole, the individual self *loses* its individuality in the Universal Self with which it is substantially one.

In contrast, the Christian asks, "What does it profit a man if he gains the whole world and *loses* himself?" (Luke 9:25). Man's highest bliss, the Hindu replies, is in the realization that Brahman-atman are identical. But how can God and man be equal? This is the question posed by Judaism, Christianity, and Islam. "Thou hast made him (man) little less than God, and dost crown him with glory and honour. Thou hast given him dominion over the works of thy hands; thou hast put all things under his feet . . . " (Psalm 8:5-6). Aren't there clear distinctions among God, man and the universe? Isn't man inferior to God yet superior to the universe? "No," says the Hindu, "God pervades everything."

> "Place this salt in water and then come to me in the morning." The son does as he is told. Uddalaka says to him: "My son, bring me the salt which you placed in the water last night."

Looking for it, the son does not find it, for it is completely dissolved. The father says: "My son, take a sip of water from the surface. How is it?"

"It is salt."

"Take a sip from the middle. How is it?"

"It is salt."

"Take a sip from the bottom. How is it?"

"It is salt."

"Throw it away and come to me."

The son does as he is told, saying, "The salt was there all the time."

Then the father says, "Here also, my dear, in this body, verily, you do not perceive Being; but It is indeed there."

Chandogya Upanishad VI.13.2

It is interesting to note that the analogies of the bees and of the rivers stress the loss of individuality, the merging of the self into the Universal Self. The analogy of the salt on the other hand illustrates the pervasive quality of Being. The Ultimate Being – That One, Brahman, God, whatever the appropriate label may be – is present in everything that exists. In other words there is in the Hindu religion no hierarchy of God, man and the universe; there is no Creator above and creatures below; no duality; only One. Brahman-atman are ultimately one; the human soul or "self" *is* the Absolute. *Tat tvam asi.*

KARMA AND SAMSARA

Karma is a technical term which means "action" in general, whether it be good or bad, ritual (religious) or secular (non-religious). Because actions invariably produce their own good and evil fruits, "a man reaps what he sows". Karma embodies this idea of moral cause and effect; in the moral sphere, every action necessitates a reaction. Therefore, the Hindu believes that his present life is the result of past karma, and that his future lives will be affected by his karma in the present existence. Thus, pain, suffering, sickness and any sort of ill-fortune is not regarded by the Hindu as an affliction sent from God (as in Islam or Judaism), nor, for that matter from Satan (as in Zoroastrianism or Christianity), but as the result of his evil karma in a past existence or existences.

The doctrine of "rebirth" to life on earth, known as *samsara*, is another distinctive feature of Hinduism.

Those whose conduct here [on earth] has been good will quickly attain some good birth – birth as a brahmin, birth as a kshatriya, or birth as a vaisya. But those whose conduct here has been evil will quickly attain some evil birth – birth as a dog, birth as a pig, or birth as a chandala [an "outcast"].

Chandogya Upanishad V.10.7

Obviously, the caste system, which was part of the social structure, acquired a kind of moral justification. If you were worthy enough to be born as a man, you were born into the caste determined by your actions in your previous life. This theory of *action-karma*, which is inextricably bound up with *rebirth-samsara*, explained, as no other doctrine could, the inequalities of birth. If a man was born a sudra, it was not because God or fate (Islam) had decreed it, but because the man had accrued "bad" karma in his previous existence and deserved no better lot. If, on the other hand, a man was born a brahmin, then obviously he had accumulated "good" karma in his previous existence. Hence, *karma-samsara* operates like a law of nature. There is no judge to whom one must account for one's actions on earth; there is no judgement to be pronounced that justifies one's eternal bliss or damnation. According to Hindu doctrine, one's future is not predestined by God (as some Christian sects believe), but determined by the eternal twin law of karma-samsara. Thus, man alone decides his own fate and is responsible for his own destiny.

Hinduism is opposed to the doctrine of eternal retribution in heaven or hell which is common to Zoroastrianism, Judaism, Christianity and Islam. "What does he know of life who only one life knows?" says a Hindu scholar. Seen from a Hindu perspective, the theory of eternal retribution is unfair. Life on earth is too short a period in which to judge the actions of any soul. A man is exposed to errors and wrong actions, either as a result of environment, or faulty upbringing, or his own genetic nature. To inflict eternal punishment upon a soul for a short span of a single life, Hinduism says, reveals a total disproportion between cause and effect; furthermore, it seems inconsistent with God's love for his created beings.

On the other hand, if one assumes that life on earth is not terminated by one existence, but, as an inevitable consequence of karma, experiences successive rebirths, then the operating natural law of karma-samsara can be regarded neither as merciful nor vindictive, but as indifferent and passionless. The Hindu is inescapably bound to this cycle of rebirth until finally he is released through the absolute destruction of individuality, the loss of self-identity or personality, and the realization that the whole universe and everything in it is an outright illusion except Brahman-atman that alone exists and is Real.

This central concept of karma-samsara evolved from a question which has preoccupied man from time immemorial: what happens after death? Not only do different religions offer different answers, but within each religion these answers seem to change into new ideas with the passage of time. Why is this so? Perhaps because what happens after death is, to the rational mind, a mere matter of conjecture; each successive age develops a more plausible theory. This evolution of ideas is true of Hinduism. The early Scriptures, such as the Rig-Veda, describe how the "soul" of the dead is carried up on high by Agni (the fire-god who consumes the body at cremation). When the soul arrives on high there is eating and drinking, various other enjoyments, reunion with loved ones and perfect, carefree bliss. In that heavenly world there are neither rich nor poor, neither the powerful nor the oppressed; no sickness or old age detract from joys that are a hundred times greater than the greatest bliss on earth. For evil doers there is an "abyss", a place which is "black-darkness".

This idea of a post-mortem judgement evolved during the later Brahmanic period. It was an idea which, during the same period, was prominent in the Iranian tradition of Zoroastrianism. Man's deeds, it was thought, were weighed in the balance after death and rewarded or punished according to the good or evil done on earth. But to certain profound thinkers these theories seemed questionable and difficult to accept, so that once again the element of doubt played a significant role in shaping a new concept.

"Who can demonstrate the experiences of the hereafter?" ask Upanishadic thinkers. "There is doubt about a man when he is dead," says an inquirer to Yama (the Death-deity), "some say that he exists; others, that he does not. This I should like to know, taught by you. . . . " (Katha Upanishad I.1.20) Yama, the God of Death, replies by first illustrating the indestructibility of the "Soul".

> The knowing Self [or Soul] is not born; It does not die. It has not sprung from anything; nothing has sprung from It. Birthless, eternal, everlasting, and ancient, It is not killed when the body is killed.
>
> If the killer thinks he kills and if the killed man thinks he is killed, neither of these apprehends aright. The Self kills not, nor is It Killed.
>
> Katha Upanishad I.2.18-19

Then Yama goes on to state the doctrine of rebirth:

Well then . . . I shall tell you about this profound and eternal Brahman, and also about what happens to the atman [soul] after meeting death.

Some [souls] enter the womb for the purpose of re-embodiment, and some enter into stationary objects – according to their work [karma] and according to their knowledge.

If a man is able to realize Brahman here, before the falling asunder of his body, then he is liberated; if not, he is embodied again in the created worlds.

Katha Upanishad II.2.6-7;3.4

Two similes vividly describe the cycle of rebirth:

Just as a leech moving on a blade of grass reaches its end, takes hold of another, and draws itself together towards it, so does the "self", after throwing off this body, that is to say, after making it unconscious, take hold of another support and draw itself together towards it.

Just as a goldsmith takes a small quantity of gold and fashions [out of it] another – a newer and better form – so does the self, after throwing off this body, that is to say, after making it unconscious, fashion another – a newer and better – form, suited to the Manes [dead and deified ancestors] or the gandharvas [demigods] or the gods, . . . or other beings.

Brihadarenyaka Upanishad IV.4.3-4

The concept of karma-samsara finally became the central concept in all Hindu thought. If living "souls" are subject to an indefinite series of lives or existences, how can one be released or liberated (*moksha* is the Indian word) from this cycle of rebirths? True, if an individual could only reach the point at which he experienced a total identification of his individual self with the Universal Self (Brahman-atman), then he would attain moksha. But how could one attain this transcending experience? The masses of people, with their religio-social caste system, were far from attaining such a blissful state. Moreover, many sensitive minds must have been profoundly depressed at the thought of such an endless, and perhaps pointless, series of rebirths. The doctrine of rebirth undoubtedly gave reassurance to those who dreaded the "abyss" or the idea of annihilation after death; but life on earth was no escape from suffering. How could one attain that realization, that true immortality, that indestructibility, that freedom from mortal existence?

The Various Paths to the Ultimate Goal

From a very early period Hinduism recognized four basic needs of human life, or lives. The first two, pleasure and wealth, are referred to as the "Path of Desire"; the last two, moral duty and liberation, as the "Path of Renunciation". Hindus do not criticize those who pursue personal pleasure, nor blame those who wish to accumulate great possessions. Nevertheless, it is thoroughly understood that neither of these needs represents the highest goals and that sooner or later in this or in some future existence (as a member of a lower caste, as an animal or as a thing) the individual must come to terms with this fact. A Hindu recognized the satisfaction of performing his duty but ultimate satisfaction can only be found in liberation from samsara – the cycle of rebirth.

While various heterodox groups (such as Jainists, Buddhists, etc.) tried to demonstrate the path towards this kind of liberation, orthodox Hindus worked out through the centuries various paths towards the same goal. Three major alternative Paths, each designed to capitalize on the nature, temperament, interests and aptitudes of the individual, evolved to match four different personality types. Some people are basically reflective; others are primarily emotional. Still others are

Sri Krishna's Temple in Mathura, Uttar Pradesh, is regarded as the site of the legendary birthplace of Krishna. Hindu pilgrims take a holy bath in the Jamuna River. (Courtesy of Government of India Tourist Office, Toronto)

characterized as empirical (they act on the basis of observation and experiment – on their own experience, not on theory), while many are essentially active. The Hindus therefore recommend different Paths for different kinds of people who wish to attain the ultimate goal of bliss.

KARMA MARGA – THE PATH OF WORKS

Karma Marga, or the Path of Works, is a methodical performance of rites, ceremonies and duties that add to one's merit. Defined for the first time in the Brahmanas, Karma Marga stipulates a "man's debts" and the means of discharging them in the following rites:

- to the deities, man owes sacrifices;
- to the seers and teachers, man owes the study of the Vedas;
- to the ancestral spirits, man owes offspring;
- to fellow-men, man owes hospitality.

The simplicity of this conception, with its emphasis on sacrificial rites, was modified with the passage of time. Gradually various codes came into existence. Typical of such law books is a collection of rules, called the Code of Manu, which was composed around 200 B.C. by a group of priests.

The Code of Manu prescribes for each separate caste a list of dietary laws, social regulations, domestic rites, public ceremonies, and religious duties. A man conducts his life by observing all the rules of his particular caste. A list of rites and ceremonies is specified for each significant episode in one's life such as birth, name-giving, initiation, marriage, and so on. Another part of the Code stipulates the honours due to the guardian dieties of the household. For example, the head of the house must see to it that such deities are properly worshipped each day and that portions of the prepared food are presented to them before each meal.

Another important domestic rite is the *shraddha* rite – the rite to ancestral spirits. The shraddha rite consists of periodic offerings of portions of food and memorial prayers. The most important food offering is the *pinda* – little balls of rice pressed into a firm cake.

The role of the women within this category can be stated very simply: to humbly serve their men.

In childhood a female must be subject to her father; in youth, to her husband; when her lord [husband] is dead, to her sons;

a woman must never be independent. She must not seek to separate herself from her father, husband, or sons. By leaving them she would make both her own and her husband's families contemptible.

Manu V. 148, 149

A faithful woman occupies herself with household duties. She respects, obeys, and worships her husband, even if he is unfaithful, virtueless, and devoid of good qualities.

Him to whom her father may give her, or her brother with the father's permission, she shall obey as long as she lives. Though destitute of virtue, or seeking pleasure elsewhere, or devoid of good qualities, a husband must be constantly worshipped as a god by a faithful wife.

Manu V. 151, 154

After her husband's death, a woman may not remarry but must remain quiet, patient, and chaste until her death. Should she violate this duty she brings disgrace to herself in this world and, instead of joining her husband in the next existence, will "enter the womb of a jackal".

She must never mention the name of another man after her husband has died. Until death let her be patient, self-controlled, chaste, and strive to fulfil that most excellent duty which is prescribed for wives who have one husband only. A virtuous wife who, after the death of her husband constantly remains chaste, reaches heaven . . . But a woman who from a desire to have offspring violates her duty toward her deceased husband, brings on herself disgrace in this world, and loses her place with her husband in heaven.

Manu V. 157-161

Many other rites and ceremonies are associated with the practice of the Karma Marga. High ethical values are also a characteristic feature of those who follow the Path of Works.

Against an angry man let him not in return show anger; let him bless when he is cursed; and let him not utter speech devoid of truth . . .

Manu VI. 48

Although it is true that many Hindus observe the "code" in minute detail even to the present day, modern conditions have forced certain changes in the ancient customs and rites. To an outsider, the Karma Marga may seem to be an exacting way of life, but to the faithful Hindu, it is an action-filled way of fulfilment and ultimately a means to liberation.

> He who thus recognizes the Self through the Self in all created beings, becomes equal minded towards all, and enters the highest state, Brahman.
>
> Manu XII. 125

JNANA MARGA – THE PATH OF KNOWLEDGE

For those spiritual aspirants who have a strong intellectual bent, Hinduism prescribes Jnana Marga, or the Path of Knowledge. Its purpose is to enable the aspirant to attain ultimate bliss through the perception of the illusory nature of names and forms and the realization of the sole reality of Brahman-atman. Naturally, only those who are of a philosophical temperament can develop a keen power of reasoning by which they can distinguish the real from the unreal, the changing from the changeless. These aspirants must cultivate such disciplines as control over the mind and the senses, which lead to inner calm, forebearance and concentration. By reasoning and uninterrupted contemplation, their ignorance gives way to the realization that the entire universe and all beings are one and the same Brahman. But to reach this ultimate realization requires long preparation and self-discipline.

The Four Stages of Life

The classical conception of the life-preparation required to reach this ultimate realization is given in the Code of Manu. Here, the Path of Knowledge and the Path of Works are interfused. Just as the year passes through four phases or seasons, and just as each day is divided into four parts – morning, noon, afternoon and evening – so does one pass through *ashramas,* or four stages in life.

STUDENT (BRAHMACARIN). During the first stage a youth leads an austere life as a celibate student, serving his teacher with humility in return for instruction, and learning sections of the Vedas. Traditionally, this stage begins between the ages of eight to eleven and lasts until the ages of twenty to twenty-three, during which time the student usually lives in the home of his teacher.

The purpose of this training is not to prepare "an encyclopaedia on two legs" but to equip the individual to cope effectively with life and to contribute to the welfare of society.

HOUSEHOLDER (GRIHASTHA). During the second stage in life, a man devotes himself to household duties. In other words, during the "noonday" stage, he marries, raises children, fulfils his duties to his family as well as to his community. Together with his wife he performs the Vedic sacrifices in accordance with the rules laid down in the Brahmanas.

FOREST-DWELLER (VANAPRASTHA). The third or "afternoon" stage in life commences when a man reaches middle-age, at which time he delegates the responsibility of the home and family to his children, while he and his wife retire into the forest in order to lead a life of reflection and meditation. He is then regarded as a "forest-dweller". The Aranyakas, "forest-treatises", prescribe various symbolic forms of worship and describe various meditations as substitutes for an actual sacrifice, since many articles and accessories required for the sacrifices are unobtainable in the forest. For example, since the worshipper needs a live horse in order to perform a Vedic horse sacrifice, the forest-dweller is instructed to follow a meditation which substitutes the dawn for the head of the horse, the sun for the eye of the horse, the air for the life in the animal, and so on. Thus, the sacrifice is lifted from the physical to the intellectual plane.

WANDERER (SANNYASIN). The fourth and last stage marks the end of a normal, regulated life for a person who lives long enough. As a sannyasin, he renounces all his former ties. Free from worldly desires and attachments, absorbed in uninterrupted contemplation, and having no fixed home, he wanders "north to the Himalayas and back south again, at home on every lake or sheet of water, as also in the infinite unbounded reaches of the sky". Having discovered complete release from every limitation, he may "neither hate nor love anything". Furthermore, he no longer need worship by means of either material articles or even mental symbols, but is simply guided by the wisdom of the Upanishads.

Various Systems of Philosophy within Jnana Marga

To the present day, the final state of absorption in the Ultimate is the goal of all worshippers who choose Jnana Marga. However, through the centuries (from about 500 B.C. to A.D. 1500) various "systems of philosophy" or *darshana* took shape. Although a great number of these systems developed, Hindus themselves have pointed out that most of them cover the same ground as any of six recognized systems.

Hindu scholars have arranged the six systems in their logical rather than their chronological order.

THE NYAYA SYSTEM. Based upon a text ascribed to a philosopher called Gautama (not Gautama the Buddha), a complete analysis of correct reasoning is attempted. The Nyaya System asserts that True or Real Knowledge is based upon four processes of knowing: sense-perception, inference, comparison of fact, and trustworthy testimony. False notions give rise to activities that have evil consequences in successive rebirths. Hence, all misery arises from false notions. Liberation, therefore, depends upon sound or true knowledge.

THE VAISHESHIKA SYSTEM. This system, founded by Kanada, applies logical methods to the study of the external world. The external world is regarded as a self-existent reality, formed by eternal and indivisible atoms eternally combining and re-combining. Later thinkers, however, declared that this process is not purely mechanistic but takes place by the power of Advishta, the divine "unseen force". All agree that alongside the eternal atoms and individual selves is an eternal Self, the source of all selves. Hence, both atoms and selves are eternally indestructible.

THE SANKHYA SYSTEM. The Sankhya System is dualistic, in sharp contrast to the doctrine that only one Being exists (Brahman-atman) expressed in the Upanishads. It maintains that there are only two real eternal categories of being: prakriti ("matter"), and purusha ("self"). Individual selves are not the product of an eternal Self but are regarded as eternal, independent and infinite. Why these selves (purushas) are associated with a body and a mind (prakriti) in one existence or life after another is an insoluble mystery associated, in some way, with karma. The self needs to be liberated from its association with matter. But the self cannot achieve this. It is in the realm of matter that the "higher intelligence" (budhi) realizes in its moment of insights the true character, or being, of the purusha. The insight destroys not only ignorance or illusion, but also matter. Hence it enables the self to realize its freedom of eternal and unearthly existence.

THE YOGA SYSTEM. The term yoga ("discipline") is used in two distinct senses. The meaning most familiar to the West is the physical, mental and psychic discipline, or technique, practised for either purely spiritual purposes or to attain maximum physical and mental, as well as spiritual, well-being. The second sense in which the word is used is to denote one of the six philosophical systems.

The greatest appeal of the Yoga system lies in its physiological and psychological measures to control the mind in an effort to concentrate.

It consists largely of special postures, controlled breathing, and rhythmical repetition of the proper thought-formulas. The claim of this system is that by controlled breathing one may control the senses. By controlling the senses one may gradually control mental processes. By controlling the activity of the mind, one may pass through a succession of stages in which the activities of the mind become more and more restricted: first, to an area of concentration, then to a restricted concentration on a single object of thought, and finally to a state of uninterrupted contemplation in which there is no distinction between the mind and its object of thought. Devoid of all mental activity, there is only pure undistracted consciousness in this final state.

Mentioned first in the Upanishads, it was given its classical form by Patanjali – probably a second century A.D. yogin. Influenced partly by the Sankhya system, Patanjali defined the Yoga system as "the suppression of the modifications of the mind". One's goal is the attainment of a state of pure consciousness, undisturbed by psychic or mental processes, or by any object of awareness. This state is known as *samadhi* – a state of trance in which the mind, "emptied of all content and no longer aware of either object or subject, is absorbed into the Ultimate and is one with the One".

The means to this goal is the eightfold *yoga*, or discipline, described in the Yoga Sutras. The first two deal mainly with ethical disciplines, such as non-violence, truthfulness, study and prayer. The next two describe right postures and controlled breathing, which, in turn, help in the practice of the next four steps associated with concentration or meditation.

The characteristic feature of Yoga in any of its forms is the discipline of the whole body in order to aid the suppression of the activities of the mind. The result is a state of pure ecstasy, of complete freedom of the "true self" from earthly bonds.

THE PURVA-MIMANSA SYSTEM. Founded by Jaimini, this system is considered to be the least philosophical of the six systems. Followers of this system are known as literalists because they cling to the literal inspiration of the Vedas. So highly did Jaimini regard the truth of the Vedas that he asserted that they never had an author; that the Vedas were uncreated and eternal, and in the language of Being Itself. Hence, the Vedas had a magical power which prevailed even over the deities.

The Vedas, and for that matter, the Brahmanas, contained the whole duty of man. By determining the literal meaning and carrying out the rites and ceremonies described in the Vedas and Brahmanas, one could attain liberation.

Although this position was not essentially altered, followers of this system declare that the duties of man prescribed in the Vedas and Brahmanas should be studied and practised as an offering to a "Supreme God", who waits to liberate his followers as a reward for their faithfulness.

THE VEDANTA SYSTEM. The name of this system derives from the Upanishads, also commonly called Vedanta, which means "the concluding portions of the Vedas". Although an attempt was first made in the first century B.C. by Badarayana to set forth the monistic teaching (the doctrine that only one Being exists) of the Upanishads in a systematic philosophical structure, it was not until centuries later that three different systems of Vedanta philosophy were founded by Sankara (ninth century A.D.), Ramanuja (twelfth century A.D.), and Madhva (thirteenth century A.D.).

Sankara's system of thought (called *advaita*, "non-dualism") holds that the world, the individual self, and Brahman, while not absolutely one, do not really exist separately and are in reality "not different". Brahman is Eternal, Undecaying, Indescribable and Impersonal. Besides Brahman, all else is transient, impure, and unsubstantial; in short, a product of "illusion" (*maya*). To regard the physical world and the individual self as "realities", (as is the common experience) is to exist in the world of "illusion". There is only One Reality, which is spaceless, timeless, and solely existent: Brahman-atman. Liberation from the cycle of rebirths comes when the "veil of ignorance" is lifted and one realizes the identity of Brahman-atman.

Three hundred years later, a diametrically opposed interpretation of the Upanishads (Vedanta) was suggested by Ramanuja. He asserted that the physical world, individual selves and the Ultimate Reality are not illusions but each real, though non-divisible, because the physical world and individual selves make up the "body" of the Ultimate Reality. In other words, the physical world and individual selves are the forms through which the Ultimate Reality is manifested. However, this Ultimate Reality is a Personal Being and not, as Sankara stated, an Impersonal Being. His name is Vishnu. He is endowed with every desirable quality: all-knowing, all-powerful, all-loving, and so on. He manifests himself in many ways. The ideal goal of men is not absorption in an Impersonal Reality, but going to "heaven to enjoy Vishnu's presence in full consciousness".

A third interpretative version of the Upanishads came through Madhva. He maintained that the individual self is neither to be identified with, nor one with, the Ultimate Reality. Furthermore, liberated selves will enjoy bliss in the presence of the Supreme Self, Vishnu. Non-liberated selves are doomed to spend eternity in hell or in endless rebirths. How is the self liberated? Through Vayu, the Wind-God, the Son of Vishnu. He is the "vehicle of the grace of God", a sort of "Holy Spirit", who "breathes His life-giving power into those whom he liberates". The echo of Christian or Muslim views, which were known in India by Madhva's time, is quite apparent in this version.

BHAKTI MARGA – THE PATH OF DEVOTION

Many people cannot be inspired by pure reasoning or rationality, but can rise to heights of spiritual elevation through devotional experiences. Often, such experiences assume the form of a passionate love of a deity, whether a god or a goddess. The most characteristic features, however, of such experiences are the surrender of self to the deity or divine being, private acts of devotion and temple worship.

Hindus attempt to make a pilgrimage at least once in a lifetime to the holy city of Varanasi (Banaras) where they take a holy bath in the waters of the Ganges. Umbrellas provide shade, while the special platforms offer places for meditation and rest. Cremation of the dead takes place at various *ghats* (steps) and the ashes are strewn on the waters. Spires and pavilions of temples are seen in the background. (Courtesy of Government of India Tourist Office, Toronto)

The first important literary record of Bhakti Marga as a true way of liberation is found in one of the great classics of religious literature, the Bhagavad Gita, which means, Song of the Blessed One. The author is unknown and the date of composition may range anywhere from 200 B.C. to A.D. 200, depending on which scholarly source one wishes to accept.

This poem is in the form of a dialogue between the warrior Arjuna and his charioteer Krishna, who is none other than the manifestation of the Supreme Deity, Vishnu, in human form. The conversation takes place just before the battle. Arjuna sees in the ranks of the opposing army a large number of his friends and kinsmen. Horror-stricken at the thought of fighting against them, he quickly lays down his weapons, preferring to be killed than to kill. Krishna, however, justifies the fight on the grounds that man's "real soul" is immortal and independent of the body; it neither kills nor is killed.

> These bodies come to an end,
> It is declared, of the eternal embodied [soul],
> Which is indestructible and unfathomable.
> Therefore fight, son of Bharata!
>
> Who believes him a slayer,
> And who thinks him slain,
> Both these understand not:
> He slays not, is not slain.
>
> He is not born, nor does he ever die;
> Nor, having come to be, will he ever come not to be.
> Unborn, eternal, everlasting, this ancient one
> Is not slain when the body is slain.
>
> Bhagavad Gita II. 18-20

In the course of eighteen chapters, the Bhagavad Gita sets forth many religious viewpoints. While it expounds Karma Marga and Jnana Marga, its pre-eminent emphasis is on Bhakti Marga, the Path of Devotion. It grants that both the Path of Knowledge and the Path of Works lead to liberation:

> In this world, aspirants may find enlightenment by two different paths:
> for the contemplative, the Path of Knowledge; for the active, the Path of Works.
>
> Bhagavad Gita III. 3

Nevertheless, the highest secret of all and the supreme message of the Bhagavad Gita is devotion:

> I am the same to all beings;
> no one is hateful or dear to me;
> those who revere me with devotion
> are in Me and I in them . . .
>
> No devotee of Mine perishes:
> for those who take refuge in Me,
> though they may be born of base origin –
> women, *vaisyas* or *sudras* –
> all attain the highest goal.
>
> Fix your mind on Me,
> Be devoted to Me,
> Worship Me, adore Me,
> And to Me you will come . . .

Bhagavad Gita IX. 29-34

The Evolution of Modern Systems of Hinduism

The Hindu masses continue to practise their traditional religious beliefs today as they did centuries ago even as the religion continues to evolve and form new branches. Not only are there millions of people who worship God in the method they best understand, but there are numerous systems that try to interpret the complexities of particular religious doctrines. One can find temples and worshippers of Brahma (deity of Creation), or of Shiva (deity of Destruction), or of Vishnu (deity of Preservation). All three, sometimes spoken of as a triad, are regarded as the manifestation of Brahman.

Of the three gods, Brahma is the least widely worshipped. Though there are less than a dozen temples dedicated to him, he is deeply respected. He is usually depicted in art as a kingly personage with four heads, riding a white goose and reading the Vedas.

Vishnu, the Preserver, is considered to be a benevolent God, and hence is very popular among the masses. The stories concerning the divine activities in the Vedas have led to his rise in popular esteem. His devotees assert that he has "come to earth" (the Indian term is *avatar* and means "descent") when he was needed. Traditionally, nine avatars of Vishnu are considered to have occurred already, while the tenth is yet to come. From the Vedas, one learns that Vishnu has appeared in the form of a dwarf to restore heaven and earth to the gods. In the

Ramayana, Vishnu appears as the prince-hero Rama, while in the Bhagavad Gita he appears as Krishna, the charioteer. In the other avatars, Vishnu appears as a fish to rescue Manu, the first man, who was being swept away in a universal flood; as a tortoise to assist the gods; as a boar to lift with its tusks the sunken earth above the depths of the sea; as a man-lion to rescue the life of a child from his demon-father; as a brahmin-hero to defeat the kshatriya caste and establish brahmin supremacy; as Gautama to establish Buddhism. His tenth avatar will be as a messiah with a sword of flame, riding on a white horse, to save the righteous and destroy the wicked at the end of this world period.

The most popular of the avatars are those of Rama and Krishna. Millions have made Rama the object of their devotion, and his image is worshipped in a way that suggests that he is the Supreme Deity. Others, however, reverentially respect Rama as an avatar of Vishnu, the Supreme Deity. Similarly, Krishna is popular both as an avatar of Vishnu (the episode of the Bhagavad Gita) and as a God. In popular folklore, Krishna is the young amorous cow-herdsman, playing on his flute melodious music, which wins him the passionate love of the *gopis* (milk-maids). He unites himself with hundreds of these adoring gopis, but his favourite is the beautiful Radha. Devotees worship either Krishna as the Supreme Deity, or seek the favour of both Radha and Krishna in the hope of being transported at death to the pleasure groves of heaven, where Krishna and Radha make love forever. Such devotees stress that "love of God" is a spiritual rather than a carnal passion.

Carvings and decorative details of Hindu temples are superb examples of ancient Indian art. They are concerned in general with the lives of gods and goddesses. Sculptures and reliefs show God Vishnu in his various *avatars* and depict scenes from various stories recorded about him. (Courtesy of Trans World Airlines)

Inside every Hindu temple, in front of the Lord Shiva, there is a Nandi - a Bull God, regarded as the carrier of Shiva. One of the biggest Nandis is outside the Temple of Chamundi Hills, Mysore, where worshippers come from time to time and make their offerings. (Courtesy of Trans World Airlines)

The third member of the Hindu triad is Shiva. His followers call him Mahadeva, the Great God. His character has some fascinating aspects, yet it is very complex. Called Rudra in the Vedas, he is "the threatener, the destroyer, the afflicter". He is the "bringer of disease and death". His presence is invariably felt at the funeral pyre. But he is not purely evil, for he can be constructive and helpful. After all, death and decay are but the prelude to new forms of *life*. Thus, Shiva stands for *Life* itself, as pure energy or force.

Hence, worshippers have come to identify the process of reproduction – in every realm of vegetable, animal and human life – with Shiva. The mystery of the cosmic and human creative force is symbolically represented by the *lingam* and *yoni* – the male and female reproductive organs. Millions of faithful believers worship these symbols in their homes as well as in their temples with devout adoration.

A distinct and fairly recent sub-division of Hinduism is the worship of Shiva's consorts, or wives, known as Shakti. Shaktism as practised today, is divided further into a "left-hand" and a "right-hand" system.

Left-hand Shaktism, represented by Durga and Kali (deities), emphasizes the black and violent side of Shakti. Its rites, which are essentially
secret and esoteric, are designed to achieve tight control of the senses
and to overcome pleasure. These rites rely heavily on what are known
as the Five Ms, namely, meat (mansa), wine (madya), fish (matsya),
parched grain (mudra) and sexual intercourse (maithuna), which are
forbidden to members of the system or sect except in the observance
of religious rites. The Five Ms are not intended as sources of gratifica-
tion or pleasure, which would be highly dangerous to the participant's
karma, but for a non-dualistic union with holy, natural force.

Right-hand Shaktism emphasizes the white and benign aspect of
Shakti. The benevolent phases of divine energy are usually considered
under the symbol of the Mother-Goddess.

Influences on Hinduism

Various religious thinkers from within as well as certain religious
movements from without have exerted their influence on Hinduism.
Sankara (A.D. 788-820) rescued Hinduism from the confusion that
attended the downfall of Buddhism in India. He re-interpreted the
Hindu Scriptures in a new light; he preached non-dualism and the
supremacy of intuitive knowledge. Then came Ramanuja (A.D. 1017-
1137), the founder of qualified non-dualism, who preached a combination of love and knowledge. Madhva (A.D. 1199-1276), in Southern
India, and Chaitanya (A.D. 1486-1533), in Bengal, both strongly ad-
vocated Bhakti Marga as the only path to liberation.

Around the fifteenth century Hinduism's contact with Islam produced in northern India such religious reformers as Kabir and Nanak,
the founders of the Sikh movement. After the British conquest of India
in the eighteenth century, the impact of Christianity shook Hinduism
to its foundation. Two movements of reform were started which succeeded to a great extent in diverting the tide of "alien faith". One was
the Brahma Samaj movement, founded by Raja Rammohan Roy (1774-
1833), which condemned image worship and the caste system, dedicated itself mainly to social reform, and worshipped the Eternal,
Unsearchable and Immutable Being, who is the Author and Preserver
of the Universe. The other was the Arya Samaj movement, founded by
Swami Dyananda (1824-1883) which was a reaction and a bulwark
against both Islam and Christianity.

The nineteenth century also saw the birth of the great Ramakrishna
Paramahamsa (1836-1886), whose spiritual experience and complete
mastery of the body and the senses won many converts to his interpretation of Hinduism. After his death his movement spread all over the

world, thanks to the efforts of his successor, Swami Vivekananda. Many religious figures, such as Mahatma Gandhi, have worked and continue working to reform from within.

Mahatma Gandhi

Mahatma Gandhi (1869-1948) represents an outstanding figure in modern India and a famous religious personality who was loved throughout the world. A brief survey of his contribution to mankind seems to be an appropriate way of ending this unit.

Born on October 2, 1869, in Porbandar, a small coastal town in Gujarat in Western India, Gandhi (usually called "Gandhiji" or "Bapu" by Indians) was the son of an important minister of a princely state. Having completed his primary and secondary education in India, he left for England at the age of nineteen to study law and soon became a barrister.

A legal case sent him to South Africa at the age of twenty-four. He lived there for the next twenty years and experienced at first hand the prejudice of "white-skinned" European settlers against "dark-skinned" people (Africans and Indians). It was this attitude and the treatment that accompanied it that persuaded Gandhi to stay in South Africa and to fight. But the method he used for fighting prejudice and discrimination was novel and significant.

Gandhi believed that violence was too great a price to pay even for fair treatment and justice. Violence, he said, always led to more violence. There was only one way to fight injustice: through non-violence. Hence, if Gandhi decided that a certain law was unfair or unjust, he considered it his duty to disregard it, cheerfully accepting the consequences without hatred and without retaliation. *Truth* and *non-violence* were the two basic values of life to which Gandhi always adhered.

Gandhi returned to India during World War I, only to find that the same situation and attitude he had resisted in South Africa existed between the ruling British officials and the Indian public. After the war, Gandhi and a few Indian national leaders challenged their countrymen to oppose British rule and what they considered was British injustice. Hundreds of thousands of men and women accepted Gandhi's call; among them was a future Prime Minister of India, Jawaharlal Nehru.

Gandhi wanted Indians to fight for their freedom, but he wanted them to achieve their goals in such a way that Briton and Indian reached new levels of understanding and became better people. To him, achieving the goals were far less important than the way they were achieved. In a world full of violence and hatred he firmly upheld the principle of non-violence.

At midnight on August 14, 1947, India (excluding Pakistan) finally won her freedom by virtue of Gandhi's two principles: truth and non-violence. Less than six months later, this "apostle of non-violence and angel of peace" died at the hands of an assassin. Three pistol shots struck him as he knelt for prayers on the evening of January 30, 1948. With his hands folded in prayer, Gandhi uttered the words, "Ram, Ram," (the name of God) and fell. Jawaharlal Nehru, by then India's Prime Minister, said of him,

> . . . the light that shone in this country was no ordinary light. It will illumine this country for many more years, and a thousand years later it will still be seen in this country.

Profoundly convinced that the best way to solve all national and international problems was non-violence, Gandhi rejected the idea that the end justifies the means. Only "pure" means, he insisted, could achieve great objectives.

In his fight against all practices which he thought unjust, Gandhi attempted to reform India's religio-social tradition of caste. "In the long history of India," says Mrs. Indira Gandhi, Prime Minister of India, "every reformer has fought against the hierarchy of caste and the debasement of women, but no one succeeded in breaking down discrimination to the extent that Gandhiji did. The women of India owe him a special debt of gratitude. And so do all other groups who suffered from age-old handicaps."

In a world of hatred, injustice and violence, Gandhi's timeless message still rings out:

> My message and methods are, indeed, in their essentials for the whole world. . . . I feel in the inmost recesses of my heart . . . that the world is sick unto death of blood-spilling. The world is seeking a way out. I believe that true democracy can only be an outcome of non-violence!

BUDDHISM

The Eightfold Way:
Buddhist symbol of life

Be ye lamps unto yourselves;
Rely on yourselves;
Do not rely on any external help.

Hold fast to the Truth as a lamp;
Seek salvation alone in the Truth;
Look not for assistance to any one besides yourselves.

Who wearies not, but holds fast to his Truth,
Shall cross this ocean of life –
Shall cease *dukkha!*

Mahaparinibbana Suttanta

BUDDHISM

Some religions are associated with geographical regions or national groups. Buddhism, like Christianity and Islam, is a world religion. Buddhism covers a huge part of Asia and the Far East: India, Ceylon, Thailand, Mongolia, Manchuria, Tibet, China, Korea and Japan. It also has many followers in Europe, Britain and North America.

Like every other religion that is discussed in this book, Buddhism explores the unknown in order to discover a universal solution to the problems of mankind. It makes the same claim: to offer a knowledge, or truth, which is final, complete and "real" life itself. Like the other major religions, it has developed profound religious philosophies and has attracted sensitive thinkers at all times and in all places throughout the world.

> The fundamental teaching of Gautama [the Buddha] . . . is clear and simple and in the closest harmony with modern ideas. It is beyond all dispute the achievement of one of the most penetrating intelligences the world has ever known.
>
> H. G. Wells

The Buddhist Scriptures

Buddhism takes its name from the title Buddha ("The Enlightened One") by which the first and most famous Buddhist leader, Siddhartha Gautama, was known. His life and teachings, as well as the principal beliefs of Buddhism, are in the Buddhist scriptures but as far as we know, the Buddha, who lived around the sixth to the fifth century B.C., wrote nothing down. Like most religious leaders, the Buddha spoke with his disciples and talked on various topics to groups of people on many different occasions. Teaching for a period of over forty years, he must have used many illustrations and answered numerous questions and problems raised by his followers.

It is not surprising, then, that as soon as the Buddha died there were many unanswered questions which led to serious differences of opinion. These differences resulted in a number of traditions and interpretations which were passed down by word of mouth for several centuries before they were committed to writing. A few more centuries passed before the so-called First Council was held, at which an agreement was reached on the selection of various materials.

The materials collected and assembled into scripture are called Tripitaka (meaning "Three Baskets") and the contents are divided into three main sections:

THE VINAYA PITAKA. This section is a collection of monastic rules for the various orders of monks and nuns and describes how the orders and disciplines were formulated, how they should be enforced, and what the Buddha had to say about them.

THE SUTTA PITAKA. This section is regarded as the most important of the three divisions, since it contains "the Gospel according to Buddha". Subdivided into numerous sections, the Sutta Pitaka contains the Buddha's discourses and sermons as well as his teachings and instructions in the form of a dialogue between the Master and his disciple. Two sub-sections in particular give an insight into the interests and character of the Buddha. Two other important sub-sections are the Dahmmapada, a collection of moral and ethical writings, and the Jataka, comprising some five hundred and fifty mythical stories, said to be the recollections by the Buddha of his previous incarnations, or former lives.

THE ABHIDHAMMA PITAKA. These writings are supposed to have been written at a later date than the other two sections. They discuss the cause and essence of all living things and are believed to supplement the beliefs described in the other collections.

According to tradition, a century after the First Council a Second Council took place to discuss the doctrines and the choice of materials in the Tripitaka. This time there was some disagreement and further Councils failed to resolve the points of difference. The result was a division between two groups of people: those who wanted to adopt the Tripitaka as it stood, and those who insisted on including more liberal materials. Forming two separate Orders (Sangha), the "liberal" group called themselves Mahasanghika (members of the great Sangha), while the "orthodox" group were called Theravadins (followers of the teachings of the Elders). Both groups, or rather, Orders, developed into main branches of Buddhism. The first group is commonly known as Mahayana (Greater Vehicle); members of the second group prefer to call their section Theravada (Doctrine of the Elders), but are referred to in a derogatory way by the Mahayana as Hinayana (Lesser Vehicle). More will be said later about these Buddhist schools.

Mahayana Buddhism developed its own canon of scriptures. Although the members of this group retained much that was included in the Tripitaka, they added other materials which contained the basis of their beliefs. As more schools and sects developed through the centuries, numerous materials were accepted as scripture. The simple truths that Buddha had once uttered would some day form the basis for some forty different sects and produce thousands of volumes of texts representing Buddhist scriptures in several different languages.

The Buddha's Early Life

The story of Buddhism must start with the story of its founder – an Indian who retained and rejected various Vedic concepts, and whose life became the cornerstone of one of the major living religions. The life of the Buddha (the Enlightened One) must be told in its traditional form, since this is the form accepted by Buddhists, who number in the millions.

If scriptural accounts of miracles and supernatural events are proofs of divine power, then the sacred books of all other religions, when they are compared with the Jataka which tells how the Buddha was born, seem very modest. Even the events leading to the birth of Jesus – the annunciation of the angels, the appearance of the star over the stable, and so on – appear commonplace compared to the vivid stories about the birth of Siddhartha the Buddha. One of these stories goes like this:

At the foot of the Himalaya mountains, on the plains of the Ganges river, there lived about twenty-five hundred years ago a clan of Indians called the Sakya clan. The ruler (*rajah*) of the Sakya clan was Suddhodana Gautama – a wealthy warrior belonging to the *kshatriya* (noble) caste.

Although Suddhodana had several wives, one of whom was Maya, the fairest maiden in the clan, he had no heir to inherit his princely throne. As Maya reached her late forties, Suddhodana began worrying about who should rule the Sakya clan. But one day, as Maya was resting on her couch she dreamed that she was carried to the top of the

Himalaya mountains and placed under a huge tree. Then she was escorted to a golden mansion. Suddenly the skies opened and a magnificent white elephant (a sign of purity in India) descended into Maya's room. With a lotus flower in its trunk, it circled around Maya three times and then struck her by the right side and entered her womb.

When Maya told her dream to Suddhodana, he called together the Hindu wise men (Brahmins) that were in his palace and asked for an interpretation. "Be not dismayed, O Rajah," they replied, "your wife will conceive by divine power and give birth to a boy – an heir. Should the boy consent to perform his household duties, he will become a universal conqueror; but should he forsake his household duties, then he will become a universal redeemer."

Hardly had they finished speaking when suddenly an earthquake occurred; in that moment many blind, deaf, dumb and lame people were miraculously cured.

While she was awaiting the birth of her child, Maya decided to visit her parents. On the way a divine voice warned her that her son would be delivered before she could reach her destination. She hurried quickly into the privacy of a garden nearby where she reached up for the support of a branch on a high tree. To her surprise the tree miraculously bowed down. Then, as she stood there, she gave birth to the infant, who was received in a golden net by four gods.

Though he was born unstained and pure, by divine conception, two streams of water – one hot and one cold – descended from heaven washing mother and child. At the same time, a boundless splendour appeared in the sky, surpassing the divine majestic lights of the gods, while angels heralded the news: "A Mighty Son has been Born!"

Simultaneously, seven other births took place in the Sakya clan: five boys, who were later to become the infant's disciples; a girl who was to become his wife; and a horse, which later featured in the unfolding stories or illustrations that he was to use.

At the same moment also, a certain wise hermit, named Asita, saw signs of divine celebration in the sky above the infant's home. He set out on foot and after a long journey came to Gautama's palace. Greatly rejoiced at the sight of the newborn child he exclaimed, "The young prince will reach the summit of perfect Enlightenment!"

Seven days after the infant's birth, Maya died and the child was left in the care of Maya's sister, who was also Suddhodana's wife. When the time came to take the baby to the Hindu temple to name him, the aunt was stunned to hear him ask her where they were going. When she told him, he obligingly agreed to go along though he recited three verses to remind her that there were no gods in any temple equal to him.

Once they were inside the temple, all the statues fell down at the infant's feet, and the Brahmins who performed the ceremony repeated the prophecy that had been proclaimed earlier; when Siddhartha, as the child was named, reached the age of thirty he would be either a conqueror or a redeemer.

Many Buddhists believe that prior to his incarnation or rebirth as Siddhartha, the Buddha had pre-existed in the Tusika (or Tushita) heaven – the fourth of six heavens of the "realm of desire". Choosing the right time, place and human channel, he had left the gods and had come to manifest ultimate reality to men on earth. Though the year of his birth is uncertain, many authorities cite 563 B.C. as a probable date. In 1956, the two thousand five hundredth anniversary of the Buddha's death was celebrated throughout Buddhist lands. By this reckoning his date of birth would have been in 624 B.C.

Many miracles are told about Siddhartha's childhood and youth, though it is impossible to cover all of them. His remarkable insight confounded his teachers. His skill in archery, which excelled all the

The principal attraction of the 20-acre area of the Po Temple in Bangkok is the reclining Buddha. It is 151 feet long, 49 feet high, and entirely covered with gold leaf. The Buddha reclines, head propped up, like a monument to relaxation. The soles of the 16-feet-long pair of feet are inlaid with mother-of-pearl, showing the 108 auspicious signs of the Buddha. (Courtesy of Trans World Airlines)

best men throughout the land, won him the right to marry a neighbouring princess named Yasodhara, who, as was mentioned earlier, was born on the day of his birth.

His father Suddhodana was so concerned over the prophecy and so anxious that his son should take over as ruler of the clan that he commanded his subjects never to let Siddhartha be exposed to any sight of suffering. Every kind of precaution was taken; three palaces and some forty thousand dancing girls were placed at his disposal, while strict orders were given that no ugliness should intrude upon courtly pleasures.

As heir to his father's wealth Siddhartha was on his way to power and prestige until, when he was about thirty years old, an event occurred which was to change his destiny and the lives of millions through the following centuries.

The Four Sights

For twenty-nine years Siddhartha was spared the sight of suffering until one day he went for a drive in his horse-drawn chariot. Naturally, this was not the first time that he had gone out for a drive into the surrounding country, but in the past, his father had sent people ahead in order to remove all signs of suffering from the young prince's route. This time, however, the plans miscarried; or, as some scriptural versions interpret the incident, a divine drama took place, and the deity was miraculously incarnated. Siddhartha saw for the first time four sights that moved him deeply:

First, he saw an old man, decrepit, broken-toothed, grey-haired, crooked, bent, trembling, and leaning on a staff.

"What is the meaning of this?" asked Siddhartha, bewildered, of his charioteer Channa.

"This comes to all men!" was the answer he received.

Then he passed a sick man, with all sorts of sores and disease, lying at the wayside.

"What is the meaning of this?" asked Siddhartha again of his charioteer Channa.

"This comes to all men!" was the reply again.

As they went farther, he met a corpse, followed by many mourners, being carried to a waiting funeral pyre.

"What is the meaning of this?" questioned Siddhartha in complete amazement.

"This comes to all men!" answered Channa.

Puzzling over the sights he had just seen, Siddhartha's attention was suddenly drawn to the serene and peaceful face of a Hindu ascetic monk, with shaven head, a tattered yellow robe and a bowl in his hand.

"What is the meaning of this?" he asked.

"This is a man who lives a homeless life in order to seek the answer to life's riddle," came the answer.

The Great Renunciation

Siddhartha was never the same after this experience. For the first time he realized the grim realities and miseries of life. He could not forget the three scenes that had revealed the nature of suffering, and the fourth, which had indicated the predicament of men who tried to escape the painful memories caused by suffering.

Haunted by the thought that the body was inescapably involved with the agony of old age, the tragedy of disease, and the sorrow of death, Siddhartha plunged into deep meditation. In vain his father tried to distract his son from his sad thoughts. Rejecting all sensual pleasures and his life of luxury, Siddhartha determined to give up his wife, his only son Rahula, his parents and his inheritance to follow the call of a "homeless truth-seeker". The prophecy was indeed being fulfilled.

Making his way late one night to where his wife and son lay sleeping, he bade them a silent farewell, afraid that if he woke them he would find it difficult to go. "When I become enlightened," he thought "I will return to see my son." Thereupon, he and his charioteer Channa left the palace and rode off towards the forest.

Reaching its edge by daybreak, Siddhartha shaved his head, changed his clothes for a ragged garment and sent his faithful charioteer back with his horse, while he withdrew into the forest in search of enlightenment. The Buddhists call his act "The Great Renunciation", for Siddhartha was now a penniless wanderer who had indeed renounced everything – home, wealth, power, family and his only son.

The Buddha

Siddhartha first joined various Brahmin teachers in order to study the Vedas. His two greatest religious masters taught him a great deal about Rajayoga and the various philosophical traditions of Hinduism. So rapidly did he advance, that soon he decided that he had learned all that the *yogins* could teach him.

His next step was to join a band of ascetics who used pain and hardship to discipline their thoughts. Siddhartha's willpower was so strong that soon no one could match the hardships he imposed on himself. At one point he allowed himself only one grain of rice a day until he was almost a walking skeleton. Siddhartha had almost starved himself to death without reaching enlightenment when he began to realize that there was no value in self-mortification because one cannot then meditate properly. He concluded that the truth was no more to be found that way than in a life of luxury.

Negative experiments are often as rewarding as positive ones. After six years of searching, Siddhartha had experienced the futility of asceticism and the disappointment of philosophic meditation – the two most popular Paths to *moksha* ("liberation"). Little did he realize that his quest was reaching its final phase.

One evening Siddhartha was sitting beneath a fig tree (commonly known as the Bo tree – short for *bodhi* or enlightenment) after promising himself that he would not rise until he had experienced the enlightenment he had been seeking for so many years. Buddhist records describe how Siddhartha was tempted while he sat under the tree in much the same way that Jesus was tempted when he was in the wilderness. Mara, the Hindu counterpart of the Devil, approached Siddhartha in the form of Desire, parading three goddesses with their tempting retinues. Siddhartha remained unmoved, whereupon Mara disguised himself as Death and tempted Siddhartha to escape his problems by committing suicide. Again Siddhartha ignored him. Finally

Daibutsu in Kamakura, Japan, was cast in bronze in A.D. 1252 and is about 50 feet tall. Pilgrims and worshippers visit and pay homage to the revered image of the Buddha. (Courtesy of BOAC)

Mara tempted Siddhartha to abandon his struggle. Siddhartha touched the earth with his finger as a sign of determination, whereupon Mara retreated. At this point Siddhartha went into a trance, passing through deeper and deeper states of consciousness and recalling his former births. He suddenly saw things clearly: the meaning of existence, the cause of suffering and the way in which release might be achieved. Siddhartha had become a Buddha (an Enlightened One).

Overjoyed by his experience the Buddha left his tree and wandered back to the place where he had left his five ascetic disciples – the men who had been born on the same day as he had. At first Mara tempted him to keep his enlightenment to himself but the selfish impulse passed, and he determined to teach suffering mankind the "truth" that he had found. It was not going to be an easy task. Siddhartha Gautama, the Buddha, was calling for a spiritual revolution. He had tested the religious beliefs of his time and had found that they did not satisfy him. He was now asking men to reject extreme asceticism and all the religious concepts associated with it.

The Buddha's First Sermon

Having found his five disciples sitting in the cool of the evening in the old Deer park, the Buddha told them he had found *the truth*. At first they doubted him, since in their estimation he had failed in his effort of physical endurance. But soon the Buddha won their confidence.

No one could have guessed that there in the old Deer park, a group of six were laying the foundation of one of the major religions of the world. There, the Buddha preached his first sermon, emphasizing the importance of the Middle Path, and explaining the Four Noble Truths and the Eightfold Way.

This sermon, which is recorded in the Vinayana-Pitika, is one of the fundamental statements about Buddhism.

> There are two extremes, O monks, that should not be prac-
> tised by one who has assumed that homeless life.
> And what are these two?
> That devoted to passions and luxury – which is low, vulgar,
> unworthy and useless; and that devoted to self-mortification
> – which is painful, unworthy and useless.

> By avoiding these two extremes, the *Tathagata* ["The Perfect
> One," referring to The Buddha] has gained the enlightenment
> of that Middle Path, which gives insight of knowledge; which
> leads to calmness, to higher knowledge and enlightenment –
> *Nirvana*.

And what, O monks, is the Middle Path, which gives insight of knowledge, which leads to calmness, to higher knowledge and enlightenment – *Nirvana?*

Truly it is the Noble Eightfold Way: right understanding, right intention, right speech, right conduct, right occupation, right endeavour, right contemplation, and right concentration.

This, O monks, is the Middle Path, which gives insight and knowledge, which leads to calmness, to higher knowledge and enlightenment – *Nirvana.*

Now this, O monks, is the noble truth of *dukkha* ["suffering"]: birth is *dukkha;* old age is *dukkha;* sickness is *dukkha;* death is *dukkha;* sorrow, lamentation, anguish and despair are *dukkha;* contact with unpleasant factors is *dukkha;* not acquiring what one desires is *dukkha.* In short, the five *skandhas* ["man's constituents"] are *dukkha.*

Now this, O monks, is the noble truth of the cause of *dukkha: tanha!* ["selfish craving, desire"] which leads to rebirth . . . *tanha* for passions; *tanha* for existence; *tanha* for non-existence.

Now this, O monks, is the noble truth for the cessation of *dukkha;* the cessation without a residue of *tanha:* abandonment; forsaking; release; non-attachment.

Now this, O monks, is the noble truth of the way that leads to the cessation of *dukkha:*
The Noble Eightfold Way: right understanding, right intention, right speech, right conduct, right occupation, right endeavour, right contemplation and right concentration.

Vinayana Pitaka

The essence of the Buddha's sermon consists of the Four Noble Truths, which he stated as follows:

All existence is *dukkha,* meaning suffering or unhappiness.
The cause of *dukkha* is *tanha;* that is to say, suffering is caused by one's selfish desire or attachment to life and everything associated with this life.

Escape from *dukkha* is possible by eliminating all selfish craving and desire – by a total rejection of life and existence.

The way to attain non-attachment, or cessation of existence,
is by avoiding the extremes of over-indulgence and asceticism;
by following the principles of the Middle Path.

The central concept of the Middle Path is the word "right" and
consists of the following Noble Eightfold Way:

RIGHT UNDERSTANDING. Having a right understanding
means perceiving and believing the Four Noble Truths.

RIGHT INTENTION. Once one has perceived and believed the
Four Noble Truths, one must renounce worldly life, accept the
"homeless" state, and follow the Noble Eightfold Path.

RIGHT SPEECH. One must act with compassion and consideration of others, abstaining from lies, slander, abuse and idle
talk.

RIGHT CONDUCT. Right conduct or behaviour means abstaining from killing, stealing, lying, committing adultery and using
intoxicants.

RIGHT OCCUPATION. One must never accept an occupation
that may be considered questionable.

RIGHT ENDEAVOUR. One must always strive after that which
is good and make a strong effort to keep away from all that is
evil or wicked.

RIGHT CONTEMPLATION. One must always learn to control
the mind in peaceful contemplation so that neither joy nor
sorrow nor any other emotion is allowed to disturb one's calm.

RIGHT CONCENTRATION. When all the other principles have
been followed, then one can reach the stage where the mind
is completely subject to one's will. One can develop the mind
to heights beyond reasoning, indeed, to *nirvana*.

Nirvana

It is difficult, if not impossible, to describe *nirvana*, since it is not simply
an intellectual goal like concentration but an experience that is indefin-
able. It is so difficult to define that even among Buddhists there is
disagreement about what *nirvana* is. The term *nirvana* literally means
"extinction" or "going out", as the light of a candle goes out when the
wax has all melted. In this sense, *nirvana* means the extinction of all
tanhas or desires. But this does not mean total annihilation. *Nirvana* is
not a state of sheer extinction, but the state in which a man when freed

from all desires and cravings feels a liberation or release from the cycle of rebirth, and hence from *dukkha*. *Nirvana* can perhaps best be described in the negative terms expressed in certain Buddhist texts.

> There is, O monks, an unborn, not made, uncompounded condition; and were it not, O monks, for this unborn, not become, not made, uncompounded condition, no release could be perceived here for what is born, has become, is made, is compounded. . . .
>
> There is, O monks, a condition where there is neither earth, nor water, nor fire, nor air, nor the sphere of infinite consciousness, nor the sphere of the void . . . that condition, O monks, do I call neither a coming, nor a going, neither a standing still, nor a falling away . . . nirvana.
>
> Samyutta-Nikaya

Thus, *nirvana* is an ultimate, peaceful bliss; and beyond this one cannot explain, since it can only be experienced. Even though the Buddhist schools may differ in their interpretations of *nirvana,* all insist that the ultimate goal of each individual is to seek it.

Anicca

Another important idea in Buddhism is the concept of *anicca* meaning "impermanence". Everything in life is transitory, passing, in constant change. Nothing is permanent. The world around and within us is in an endless process of change and decay, of coming and going, like the turning of a wheel.

No modern scientist would question this view. Geologists confirm that the "everlasting" mountains and hills are continually being worn away; that given time, valleys will become hills, and hills will become valleys. Similarly, biologists speak of the "dynamic equilibrium" of man, by which they mean that an individual's chemical components change from moment to moment. The gradual, physical change that takes place in the human, animal, or plant kingdom needs no further confirmation nowadays. Few, if any, would disagree that the elements that make the universe and everything within it have no permanence.

Buddha stated that all existence is *dukkha* and that no man can escape suffering; but he also indicated that all existence is *anicca* and that everything is subject to change.

These insights were expressed by Buddha twenty-five hundred years ago. Though these two ideas challenged the religious views of most people during Buddha's lifetime, men have ever since echoed the validity of these two universal facts. A short but interesting narrative, recorded in the Buddhist scripture, illustrates the significance of these two important principles.

> Once Gotami, an Indian woman, came to the Buddha crying, "O Exalted One, my only son has died. I went to everyone and asked, 'Is there no medicine to bring my son back to life?' And they replied, 'There is no medicine; but go to the Exalted One, he may be able to help you.' Can you, O Exalted One, give me medicine to bring my only son back to life?"
>
> Looking at her compassionately, the Buddha replied, "You did well Gotami, in coming here for medicine. Go, and bring me for medicine some tiny grains of mustard seed from every house where no one – neither parent, child, relative, nor servant – has died."
>
> Gotami, delighted in her heart, went away to fetch as many tiny grains of mustard seed as she could find. From one house to the other, she moved frantically all day long, as each time she was told, "Alas! Gotami, great is the count of the dead in this house."
>
> Overcome with exhaustion, she finally went to the burning-ground outside the city with her dead son in her arms. "My dear little boy," said she, "I thought you alone had been overtaken by this thing which men call *death*. But now I see that you are not the only one, for *this is a law common to all mankind.*" And so saying, she cast the little corpse into the fire.
>
> Then she sang:
> No village law, no law of market town,
> No law of a single house is *this* [death].
> Of all the world, and all the worlds of gods,
> This only is law: *All things are anicca.*
>
> When she returned to the Buddha, she was greeted by him. "Gotami, did you get the tiny grains of mustard seed for medicine?"
>
> "Done, O Exalted One, is the business of the mustard seed! Only give me refuge."

All that exists is *anicca* and is subject to the changes which occur through the cycle of birth, growth, decay, and death. To crave or desire life (*tanha*) is to go through this process; and this process is *dukkha.* Even death, the Buddhists believe, is only one point in the cycle of change: it does not mark the end of existence. *Nothing* is permanent, unchanging, eternal or immortal.

Anatta

Nothing eternal or immortal? What about the age-old belief in man's immortal soul? Is there not an eternal, immortal entity in man called "soul" or "self"? What about an eternal God or gods? Is he (she, it, or they) not unchanging?

These are important points in Buddhism but the Buddha's teaching is not clear on these issues. Though various schools within Buddhism differ on certain minor points, they tend to agree on the following viewpoints.

Man is not made up of two entities, a "soul" and a "body", of which the body is perishable and the soul imperishable and immortal. Man is made up of five components, or *skandhas,* as they are usually called: physical characteristics, perceptions, feelings, subconscious predispositions, and awareness (or consciousness). The union, or rather, the interplay of these five components constitutes what is known as the "individual".

Each component, however, is in a state of perpetual change, and at death the union or interplay disperses only to pass to a new existence, just as a candle flame can be transferred from one wick to another. Hence, there is no permanent reality inside or outside man, except the reality of the ceaseless state of *being.*

Being is one and indivisible; but the ever-changing forms are innumerable and perishable. What is known as the "self" or "individual" is merely the name given to an appearance: that of the interplay of the five *skandhas.* But how does being transmigrate, or pass from one existence to the other? Several centuries after the Buddha, the matter was explained in the following way:

> "How does rebirth take place without anything transmigrating?" asked the king to the wise one.
>
> "Suppose, your majesty, a man was to light a candle from another candle-light; please tell me, does the one light transmigrate to the other light?"
>
> "Of course not! O wise one."
>
> "In exactly the same way does rebirth take place without anything transmigrating, your majesty."
>
> "Give me another illustration, O wise one!"
>
> "Do you remember, your majesty, learning poetry or verse from your teacher when you were a boy?"
>
> "Yes, indeed . . . "
>
> "Please tell me, your majesty, did the poetry transmigrate to you from your teacher?"

"Of course not! O wise one."

"In exactly the same way does rebirth take place without anything transmigrating, your majesty."

Thus, there is no permanent "self" or "ego" (*anatta*) in the five *skandhas* which make up the personality. Nor is the self or ego immortal. In other words, there is no permanent self or ego or soul that moves from one existence to another. Just as the light of a candle does not transmigrate from one candle to another, so the soul or self of an individual does not transmigrate from one body to another. There is no permanent, unchanging, immortal soul that moves from one material form into another. Herein lies the difference between Hinduism and Buddhism. While the former affirms that the soul (*atman*) was eternal and immortal, moving from one perishable material form to another until *atman-Brahman* was realized, the latter flatly denies the idea of a separate body and soul, let alone the immortality of the soul.

Nowhere, however, does the Buddha deny the *existence* of an ego or self. What he does teach is that no *permanent* entity – which is not subject to *anicca* and *dukkha* – exists in any of the human faculties. Whatever characteristics happen to be a part of any one individual cannot be eternal or immortal, because they are subject to *anicca*.

The Buddha and Indian Religion

The Buddha challenged many Indian religious views and rejected the two most fundamental paths of salvation in Hinduism: the philosophical path (Jnana Marga) and the devotional path (Bhakti Marga). Salvation for the Buddha (and for Buddhists) meant cessation of *tanha*, not the union of *atman-Brahman*. True, the goal of both the Buddhist and the Hindu was release from the cycle of birth and death but the Hindu proposed that the realization of the oneness of *atman-Brahman* would lead to liberation from rebirth, while the other proposed the extinction or cessation of *tanha*.

Not only do Buddhists and Hindus differ about the nature of salvation and the way of reaching it but they also disagree about a belief in god or gods. Buddhists argue that gods and goddesses, if they exist, are subject to *anicca* – change and impermanence. The so-called gods of Hinduism are no more immortal than the men who worship them, according to the Buddhists. Hence, to offer sacrifices, rituals and prayers is useless. "Could the farther bank of the river Akirvati," the Buddha would say, "come over to this side, no matter how much a man prayed for it to do so?" Obviously not. And for similar reasons, the Buddha placed no value on the Vedas – the Hindu scriptures – nor on any form of ritual, prayer, or worship. Moreover, with no gods and no sacrifices there was no need for the priests, the Brahmins.

At one stroke, therefore, Buddha challenged the traditional superiority of the Brahmin caste and the age-old belief in *atman-Brahman* with all its structures of salvation. Buddha saw no place for a god or gods, and he rejected the idea that man possessed an eternal soul. By challenging the idea of the soul, Buddha also made nonsense of the Hindu law of *karma-samsara* and the whole structure of the caste system.

To reject the belief in gods and in *atman-Brahman* was bad enough, but to deny the aristocratic prestige of the Brahmin caste and the caste system was to strike a severe blow at the core of Hinduism. Inevitably it invited the hostility of the most powerful group within Hindu society. No wonder that Hinduism regarded, and still regards, Buddhism as a heresy.

According to Buddha, if a man belonging to any caste experienced a "change of heart" and altered his ways, he would escape the full consequences of the evil committed in his previous existences. There would be no more necessity to move up or down the Hindu scale to pay for one's past *karma*. If, on the other hand, an individual continued in his "old way" of *tanha*, then his desire for existence had not been extinguished, and hence, would be reborn. Here, it must be remembered that no individual permanent entity passed from one existence to the other, except the flow of being. Only he who had no craving or desire for existence could free himself from future rebirths.

How could one be released from the cycle of rebirths? No god or gods are necessary. No worship, no sacrifices, no ritual or prayers will ever attain this goal. Man *alone* can stop this process of rebirth. Each individual has to rely upon himself, and on his own powers. No one can be released from the cycle of rebirths except by his own unaided efforts. Here is the Buddha's final message to his disciples:

> Therefore . . . be ye lamps unto yourselves; rely on yourselves; and do not rely on any external help! Hold fast to the Truth [The Four Noble Truths] as a lamp! Seek salvation alone in the Truth. Look not for assistance to any one besides yourselves!
>
> Be earnest then . . . be steadfast in resolve. Keep watch over your own hearts. Who wearies not, but holds fast to his Truth, shall cross this ocean of life – shall cease *dukkha*!
>
> Mahaparinibbana Suttanta

Since the Buddha rejected most of the features commonly associated with religion, many have regarded Buddhism as a sort of "atheistic" or "non-theistic" religion. At best Buddhism may be regarded by some people as the earliest and strictest form of "humanistic" religion which directs man to find his own salvation. Though Atheism and Humanism are two popular philosophies in modern, western society, few people would define them as religions. The validity of calling Buddhism a religion, however, has never been disputed.

Sangha
The Buddha was not able to win over his disciples immediately but once they understood his views, the Buddha and the five wandered through northern India preaching the message of the Middle Path. Many converts, especially from the Buddha's own caste – the Kshatriya – followed them, and within three months the number of disciples rose to sixty.

As early as the Buddha's time the missionary aspects of the movement can be illustrated by the traditional saying of the Buddha, as he sent the sixty disciples in all directions to preach the Middle Path:

Interior of the Wat Benchamabopit Temple, also known as Marble Temple, in Bangkok, Thailand. Worshippers gather to pay homage to the revered golden image of the Buddha. Flowers, incense, and prayers are usually offered. (Courtesy of BOAC)

Go ye forth, O disciples, for the salvation and joy of many, out of compassion for the world. . . . Go not two together on the same path. Preach, O disciples, the doctrine which is noble in its beginning, in its course, and in its consummation . . .

Proclaim the Noble Path!

Samyatta Nikaya

Soon the number of followers multiplied. Not only Kshatriyas but many Brahmins, as well as members of the lower castes, joined the group. During the dry season, when they could travel easily, they went about separately converting many Hindus, but during the three rainy months when travelling was almost impossible even for men on foot, they lived together in a monastic life of self-discipline. This communal life during the rainy months developed into a monastic Order, called the Sangha. After a time, perhaps even after the Buddha's death, a definite pattern of rules and regulations evolved – the wearing of a yellow robe, the shaven head, the carrying of a begging bowl, the daily methods of meditation, and the vow made by a newcomer. The vow consisted of a three-point statement:

I take refuge in the Buddha;
I take refuge in the Dhamma;
I take refuge in the Sangha.

This creed simply meant that a convert accepted, as his spiritual guide, the Buddha, the Buddha's teaching (*Dhamma* means the "Truth"), and the monastic Order which the Buddha had founded. In addition, all members of the Sangha undertook to abide by the following precepts or rules:

1. Refrain from destroying life: do not kill.
2. Refrain from taking what is not given: do not steal.
3. Refrain from unchastity: do not be unchaste.
4. Refrain from bearing false witness: do not lie.
5. Refrain from using strong drinks: do not use intoxicants.

Five additional rules were to be observed by all newcomers especially and by all Buddhist monks on special festive occasions.

6. Eat moderately, but not after noon.
7. Do not look at dancing, singing, or drama.
8. Do not use perfumes, scents, cosmetics, or ornaments.

9. Do not use comfortable beds.
10. Do not accept gold or silver.

These "Ten Commandments" of Buddhism illustrate the Middle Path. On the one hand they call for the rejection of self-indulgence and of the pleasures of life, while on the other, they stop short of demanding extreme asceticism.

From time to time disputes broke out among the members of the Sangha. At first the Buddha simply lectured the disciples to end their quarrelling and warned them about the dangers of division. His general remarks were ignored until quarrels led to angry words and even blows. The result was the Buddha's classical story of Prince Dirghayu:

> In former times, there lived at Benares a powerful king whose name was Brahmadatta of Kashi. One day he went to war against King Dirgheti of Kosala.
>
> When King Dirgheti saw that resistance was impossible, he left his kingdom and fled away. Wandering from place to place, he finally came to Benares and lived in disguise with his wife, the queen, outside the town in a potter's house.
>
> Soon his wife bore him a son, and they called him Dirghayu.
>
> When Dirghayu had grown up and received a good education from his father, Dirgheti sent him away fearing lest all three might be found out and killed.
>
> One day, the former barber of King Dirgheti, who had now come to Benares, saw and recognized his master. Being of evil nature, he betrayed King Dirgheti to King Brahmadatta.
>
> When King Brahamadatta heard of the fugitive king, he ordered him and his wife to be bound and executed.
>
> While the captive king and queen were led through the streets of Benares to the place of execution, he met his son. Careful not to betray the presence of his son, yet anxious to communicate to him a last advice, he cried: 'O Dirghayu! Do not look long, do not look short, for hatred is not appeased by hatred; hatred is only appeased by renouncing hatred.'
>
> After the execution, Dirghayu bought some strong intoxicants and, by offering them to the guards, made them drunk. Then he took the bodies of his parents and laid them upon a funeral pyre and burned them with all the religious rites and honours.
>
> When King Brahmadatta learned of this, he was afraid lest Dirghayu find a favourable occasion and take revenge for the death of his parents.

Soon Dirghayu offered his services, and was engaged in the royal elephant stable. Winning his way through the castle, he was entrusted with a responsible position in serving the king.

One day, during a hunting expedition, King Brahmadatta and Dirghayu were left alone. Tired from the game, the king laid his head upon his servant Dirghayu whom he trusted.

Now Dirghayu unsheathed his sword, and thought: 'This king has done us great injury; he is now in my power.' But the last words of his father kept repeating in his mind: 'Hatred is not appeased by hatred; hatred is only appeased by renouncing hatred.' And so he put his sword back into the sheath.

Restless and frightened, the king awoke from his sleep. When Dirghayu asked why he looked so frightened, the king said, 'My sleep is always restless because I often dream that young Dirghayu will come upon me with his sword.'

Drawing his sword, the young lad said, 'I am Dirghayu, the son of King Dirgheti, whom you have robbed of his kingdom and slain together with the queen, my mother; the time for revenge has come.'

The king, seeing himself at the mercy of King Dirgheti's son, raised his hands and cried: 'Grant me my life, O Dirghayu; grant me my life.'

Then Dirghayu replied without any ill-feeling or bitterness. 'O king, how can I grant you your life, since my life is endangered by you. You, O king, must grant me my life.'

'Then grant me my life,' said the king, 'and I will grant you yours.' And there the two made an oath.

When they returned from the hunt, the king asked Dirghayu to explain his father's last words. 'O king, you have killed my father and mother. If I should deprive you of your life, then your partisans will deprive me of mine, and again, my partisans will deprive your partisans of theirs. Thus, hatred is not appeased by hatred. But now, O king, you granted me my life and I yours. Thus, hatred is appeased by renouncing hatred.'

Then the king returned to Dirghayu his father's kingdom and gave his daughter to him in marriage.

"Now, O monks," concluded the Buddha, "if such can be the forgiveness and forebearance of kings, how much more must you so let your lights shine before the world, that you are seen to be forgiving and forebearing. Enough, O monks! No contentions, no disputes, no divisions!"

During his forty-five years of active ministry, the Buddha was asked several times to consider an Order for women. With many reservations and much reluctance, he finally consented, but his opinion of the monastic order for women is implied in his remarks to his cousin Ananda, who was a close and devoted disciple.

> If, Ananda, women had not received the permission to enter the Order, the pure religion would have lasted long, the good law would have stood fast for a thousand years. But since they have received permission, it will stand fast for only five hundred years.
>
> Maha-Parinibbana

After a long lifetime of teaching and preaching, the Buddha died at the age of eighty (483 B.C.). His calm and gentle spirit, his self-sacrificing life and his love for mankind were largely responsible for the continued expansion of Buddhism. The development of Buddhism was no exception to the general rule that religious movements undergo considerable change after the loss of their founder or leader. Various questions, such as what was the way one could attain *nirvana,* arose at many points, and opinions differed widely. Serious differences split the Sangha into a number of groups. For several centuries there was no agreement about the oral traditions which ought to be included in a collection of scriptures. After centuries of disputes and of discussions held in a number of councils, the Sangha as a whole divided into two different schools: the Hinayana (Lesser Vehicle), also known as Theravada (Doctrine of the Elders), and the Mahayana (Greater Vehicle).

The Rise and Spread of the Two Schools

Little is known about the spread of Buddhism immediately after the death of the Buddha. But a little over two hundred years after his death, about 270 B.C., there came to the throne of India one of the most remarkable figures in Indian history – King Asoka. Asoka was the grandson of an army officer who had defeated Alexander the Great's forces when they were stationed in India. Like his grandfather, and later his father, Asoka continued to expand the imperial territory.

One day, however, he suddenly revolted against the idea of war. Turning to the teaching of Buddha, he accepted the new faith, opposed war, and refrained from the use of arms. The effect of his conversion was tremendous, and under his royal patronage the Buddha's teaching soon spread throughout his empire.

Converted to peace by the horrors of war, Asoka became an ardent promoter of *Dhamma* (Moral Teachings or the Truth). He called upon his subjects and neighbouring countries to accept and follow the practical morality of his new faith: brotherly kindness to all living creatures, practice of justice and truth, and an endeavour to attain the "higher" life.

He set an example by building hospitals for the care of his people, by digging walls and planting trees, by promoting the education of all, and by carving the guiding principles of his faith upon numerous monuments. Archaeologists are still finding traces of the temples he built and other legacies of his conversion.

He is best remembered, however, for his missionary work. He sent imperial missionaries, not only throughout his vast domain, but to all parts of India and as far west as the Hellenized kingdoms of Asia, Syria, Egypt and Europe. The most important of these foreign missions were to Ceylon and Burma. These two countries along with Thailand (Siam), which probably joined the Buddhist fold around the fifth to the seventh century A.D., have faithfully preserved the essential teachings of the Buddha according to the traditions of the Hinayana (or Theravada) school.

It was probably during Asoka's reign, and certainly within a hundred years after his death, that several factors led finally to the division of Buddhism into two major groups: the Mahayanists, the liberals, and the Hinayanists, the traditionalists. The terms *Mahayana* and *Hinayana* were invented by the Mahayanists to denote that, contrary to the orthodox attitudes of the Hinayanists, the religious outlook of the Mahayanists was broad enough or "large" enough to include all mankind in their vision of salvation. This led to doctrinal differences between the two schools, as we shall later see.

During the first century B.C., however, Mahayana Buddhism reached China (during the Han dynasty) and by the first century A.D. Indian Buddhist missionaries introduced the Buddhist scriptures. An attempt was made to translate the texts into Chinese. Several centuries later the Buddhist religion had intermingled with the two famous existing systems, Confucianism and Taoism.

Sometime during the fourth century A.D., Buddhism entered Korea through China; and around the sixth century A.D. penetrated Japan, first through Korea, and later, with far more impact, through China. A century later, Buddhism reached Tibet (possibly from China) where it was grafted to the native religion to develop a character quite different from that of any other country. The form of Buddhism that took root in Tibet is usually referred to as Lamaism, and has a centralized hierarchical system with the Dalai-Lama acting as the Head or "Pope",

The Wat Phra Keo Temple, also known as the Temple of the Emerald Buddha, was built in A.D. 1784 by Rama I, the first king of Bangkok, Thailand. The outer walls and columns are covered with porcelain mosaic, the doors are resplendent with inlays of mother-of-pearl, and the spires are covered with gold leaf. Surrounding the temple are dozens of pagodas and pavilions, and a whole mythology of gods, goddesses, and guardian spirits. Towering masked figures, about 20 feet high, stand watch by the entrance gates. (Courtesy of Trans World Airlines)

and worshipped as an incarnation of Bodhisattva. A *bodhisattva* is one who has attained enlightenment (*bodhi*) as to the nature of his essence (*sattva*) but out of compassion towards humanity goes about to share his joy and enlightenment with other fellow-men. Mahayana Buddhism, then, spread northward into China, Korea, Japan, Tibet and Viet Nam, while Hinayana Buddhism, the Buddhism of the orthodox school, expanded southward into Ceylon, Burma, Thailand (Siam), Cambodia and Laos.

Meanwhile, Buddhism was encountering difficulties in its country of origin – India. There were several reasons for the decline of Buddhism in India, but one of the basic reasons was that it was absorbed back into Hinduism. While it had spread throughout the Far East by the sixth century A.D., it was beginning to decline in India. By the thirteenth century A.D., because of the Islamic invasion, it had practically disappeared from India, and today, very few Buddhists are found there.

Differences Between the Two Schools

Many differences in belief are the result of national and cultural variations, as seen, for example, in the Buddhism of China, Japan or Tibet.
Moreover, the farther Buddhism spread in time and space from its
centre of origin, the more profound was its transformation. Before
discussing any distinctive features, the following precaution from one
of the modern Buddhist scholars, D.T. Suzuki, should be borne in
mind:

> There are not two Buddhisms. The Mahayana and the
> Hinayana are one, and the spirit of the founder of Buddhism
> prevails in both. Each has developed in its own way, according
> to the difference in environment in which each has thriven and
> grown, understanding by environment all those various fac-
> tors of life that make up the peculiarities of an individual or
> nation.

Temple of the Sacred Tooth in Kandy, Ceylon, houses a tooth of the Buddha. A
colourful festival honours the sacred tooth of the Buddha every August. Two saffron-
robed monks stand in front of the temple. (Courtesy of Trans World Airlines)

Todaiji Temple in Nara, Japan, was founded in A.D. 745 and is well known for its Daibutsu - a colossal image of the Buddha (160 feet high, 187 feet long, and 166 feet wide) in the act of preaching a sermon. (Courtesy of Japan Information Centre, Toronto)

Let us briefly examine the more general differences which distinguish the two main schools one from another.

The two chief differences between the Theravadins (a term which is more acceptable to them than Hinayanists) and the Mahayanists lie in their concept of the Buddha and in their general view of man and his salvation. All Buddhists look back to the Buddha as the great Master and living embodiment of the religious ideal they seek to realize. Similarly, all agree that suffering and unhappiness (*dukkha*) constitute the basic core of existence; that once the cause of *dukkha* is realized to be *tanha,* then *tanha* can be brought under control in order to gain release from future births. But this is where the differences start.

When the Theravadins speak of their Master, they mean the *human* Gautama, who renounced all worldly interests and pursuits so that he could find a way of escaping from the suffering involved in the transitory forms of existence. They regard him as the Enlightened One; a great man; but still a man. By complete detachment, Gautama, the Buddha, pioneered the search for the blissful peace of *nirvana* and found it; he set an inspiring example for anyone who wanted to follow his lead. But the Theravadins believe that neither he, as the Buddha, nor anyone else (god or gods) can save his fellow seekers.

In other words, the Buddha's entrance to *nirvana* was the direct result of *his own* achievement; it cannot bring *nirvana* to others. Each individual seeker should follow the Buddha's example by accepting the "homeless" state in which Buddha lived; but ultimately, the individual must know that he cannot receive any help for his salvation except from himself. If a person is to achieve release from rebirth and find *nirvana*, he must do it by his own efforts. The Theravadins think of Buddha as the first man who attained salvation by his own efforts, and the man who passed his knowledge of the Middle Path on to his fellow man. Every individual, they believe, can attain the same salvation by his own effort and self-discipline.

The Theravadin believes that ideally one should renounce worldly pursuits and interests, join the "homeless" state of a monk, and strive to reach *nirvana*. Such an ideal person is regarded as an *arhat* (a worthy person), who lets nothing distract him from his ultimate goal. Naturally, not everyone is sufficiently free of obligations and responsibilities to reject everyday life in favour of the "homeless" state. Hence the Thervadin sect is referred to as the "Small Vehicle" or Hinayana school.

The Mahayanists, on the other hand, see their Master as more than the human Gautama; they see him as an incarnation of an *eternal* Buddha-nature – the manifestation in human form of an Eternal Essence. They see Gautama as one among several incarnations of this Eternal Essence, which they believe has always existed in all ages and in innumerable worlds for the salvation of all beings. Gautama was the fourth of these incarnations, but the most significant of them all. Gautama himself prophesied that there was one more Buddha to come, referred to as *maitreya*.

Mahayanists maintain that it was out of *compassion* for others that the Buddha entered this world of existence in order to aid others towards salvation. He was willing to postpone his own entrance into *nirvana* in order to help others attain it too.

Among Mahayanists, anyone, theoretically speaking at least, may aspire to *nirvana* without necessarily accepting a "homeless" state. The ideal person is not the *arhat* but the *bodhisattva* – one who, out of compassion, vows and dedicates his life to the welfare of mankind by delaying his entry into *nirvana*.

Though broadly speaking these are the major differences between the two schools, the "liberal" attitude of the Mahayana school contributed to the gradual development of many sects and many versions of Buddhist belief. For instance, the idea that the Eternal Essence was incarnate in Gautama introduced the deification and worship of Gautama himself; the idea that the ideal man was the *bodhisattva* who stood at the threshold of *nirvana* only out of compassion for mankind led to a special status for such men – the status of "saviours". This belief in the special significance of the *bodhisattva* created a vast number of them who became objects of public prayer, worship and of faith and devotion. In turn, images were introduced to help in the worship of the *bodhisattvas*. These developments led to a form of polytheism and to the belief that the way to salvation was through faith in Gautama the Buddha. Vivid portrayals of heaven and hell were developed that appealed to the masses.

Varieties of Mahayana Buddhism

The character of Mahayana Buddhism varies a great deal from sect to sect. Since there are so many of them, only three of the best known sects are described briefly.

THE PURE LAND SECT. This sect was founded in China in the fourth century A.D. by a Chinese converted to Buddhism. In the twelfth century A.D. a Japanese convert introduced this sect to Japan, where it is now known as the Jodo school.

The emphasis of this school is on salvation by faith in Amitabha. (O-mi-to in Chinese, and Amida in Japanese). Traditionally, O-mi-to was once a king who renounced his title, became a monk and later took the vow of a *bodhisattva*. Out of his infinite compassion and by the power of his accumulated merit, he called into existence the domain called Sukhavati, the "Western Paradise", or, as it is generally known, "the Pure Land". According to the Pure Land Sect, all who are ensnared by desire (*tanha*) or ignorance, but who sincerely call upon the name of O-mi-to, are reborn in the Western Paradise, where they can continue the process of liberation under happier and more encouraging conditions than they can in this existence. The Pure Land, then, is not the goal, but a stepping-stone to the goal; nor is it a place for purification like purgatory which among Christians is regarded as an intermediate state before a soul is accepted in heaven. The Pure Land is simply a place where one can receive, under favourable conditions, liberation from the cycle of bodily existence.

A devotee who merely repeats the sacred name of O-mi-to unceasingly is assured of reaching the Pure Land:

Namu O-mi-to Fu	(Chinese version)
Namu Amida Butsu	(Japanese version)
Hail Amitabha Buddha	(English version)

Shown above, the tea ceremony in Japan is practised as a means of improving one's spiritual qualities in cultivating unity of body and mind. Utensils used for the tea ceremony are shown below. (Courtesy of Japan Information Centre, Toronto)

It is easy to understand why such a simple, straightforward belief became popular among a majority of the masses. Mahayana Buddhism also gave birth to contemplative movements for people who required more philosophical, sophisticated beliefs.

THE CH'AN OR ZEN SECT. According to tradition this school was introduced by Bodhidharma, an Indian Buddhist, who may have come to China around the sixth century A.D. In fact, the term *Ch'an* or *Zen* means "meditation" in Chinese and Japanese respectively. The sect established itself in Japan in three separate waves during the twelfth, thirteenth and seventeenth centuries A.D.

According to a generally accepted legend, the Emperor sent to Bodhidharma when he came to China. During their interview, the Emperor asked Bodhidharma: "How much merit would I accumulate if I were to donate to the Buddhist Order and encourage the translation of the sacred books?" "No merit at all!" was the blunt reply. "No merit is accumulated from good works; reading scriptures is useless and worthless; only inward meditation is the path to enlightenment." And to demonstrate to the sceptical Emperor what he meant, Bodhidharma is said to have gone to Mount Su where he sat facing a wall in meditation for the next nine years.

Whatever the origin and circumstances of this story, Ch'an or Zen Buddhism does not accept institutionalized expressions. It has no set

The exchange of nuptial cups in a Japanese Shinto wedding ceremony, where the bride and groom drink *sakee* (a kind of wine made from rice). (Courtesy of Japan Information Centre, Toronto)

Novitiate temple girls performing the sacred sword dance during the Yayoi Festival - an annual celebration in March of the Futaarasan Shrine. (Courtesy of BOAC)

pattern and absolutely rejects the deification of the Buddha. A frequently quoted expression of this sect is, "If you meet the Buddha, kill him." The quotation implies that the Buddha was a man, not a god, and never wished to be worshipped; it also implies that there is a meditative awareness greater than Buddhahood.

Soon people devoted themselves to the practice of *zazen* (meaning "sitting in meditation") in order to achieve *satori* (enlightenment). To promote the experience of *satori*, the technique of the *koan* ("riddle") was employed. The *koan* is a riddle, or problem, which cannot be solved by the intellect and is set by a Zen master to the student. It is designed to heighten and develop the intuitive faculty of a disciple until he reaches beyond reasoning and attains *satori*. Later, there developed a split within Zen Buddhism on the question of whether one experienced a gradual *satori* or a sudden *satori*.

One of the favourite *koans* generally introduced to a new disciple is, "What was your original face before your parents begot you?" There are hundreds of different *koans*, each designed to probe beyond the grasp of reasoning. Here are a few popular ones: "All things return to the One; what does the One return to?" "If clapping two hands produces a sound, what is the sound of one hand clapping?"

Obviously, no logical answer is expected to any of the *koans*. The whole purpose is to realize one's own Buddha-nature, to accept the limitations of human reasoning and to probe beyond the barriers of rational thinking to insight. If a learner persists on reasoning by asking further questions, then the Zen Master may kick him, slap him, or even throw him down. This treatment is justified for the sake of breaking the learner's hold on reason.

THE ESOTERIC SECT. This sect appeals to people who are not attracted by philosophy or by movements of a pious nature so much as they are drawn by mysticism and mysterious rites. Buddhist mystery schools first emerged in India in the sixth century A.D., then in China during the eighth century A.D. and a century later in Japan. The chief feature of these schools is their reliance upon Buddhist *bodhisattvas* (saviours), male and female, whose help is solicited through appropriate rituals. These rituals fall under the three "M" groups:

> MUDRA: various symbolic gestures made by the hands and fingers.
> MANTRA: formulae of an esoteric nature based on scientific knowledge of the occult power of sound.
> MANDALA: visual aids, such as picture charts, diagrams and magical circles, to help the devotee in acquiring a mystical union with the particular *bodhisattva*.

The Jidai Matsuri Festival (October 23) is performed annually by Japanese Shinto devotees. The Ark represents the presence of God and is carried through the streets. (Courtesy of Japan Information Centre, Toronto)

Before they are allowed to share the more important secrets of the sect, devotees go through a preliminary training period. This consists of thousands of prostrations, breathing patterns, repetitions of mystical formulae in a precise sound pattern and the preparation of symbolic sacrifices. Each *bodhisattva* is represented by certain symbols and formulae peculiar to himself or herself. By performing these rituals, the devotee is gradually able to identify himself with a particular *bodhisattva* and become one with him or her. Some of the mystical rites consist of elaborate rituals to the accompaniment of music. Secret formulae, symbols and visualisations are all interpreted gradually to the disciples as their insight into the mystical nature of the *bodhisattva* grows deeper.

These three sects are not the only ones; there are dozens of other Buddhist sects and sub-sects. Nevertheless, each school of Buddhism in its own distinctive way proclaims the Truth as once taught by their Master, the Buddha.

ZOROASTRIANISM

Fire-urn:
Symbol of Ahura Mazdah's power

O Ahura Mazdah . . .

Reveal unto me for my enlightenment that which Thou hast ordained as the better path for me to follow, so that I may join myself unto it . . .

Yasna 31.5

ZOROASTRIANISM

The preceding chapters have outlined and attempted to explain the development of some of the most widespread modern religions. This chapter is concerned with Zoroastrianism, a religion that, in modern times, has few adherents.

The reason for including Zoroastrianism in a study of world religions is that its influence in ancient times was so great and so widespread that no modern religion has been untouched by it. At the height of its glory in ancient Persia, it concerned itself with occultism, magic, divination, alchemy, astrology and almost every form of discipline which attempted to distinguish what is good and what is evil. It regarded life as a continual battle between good and evil, and hence its quest for goodness and truth was an indispensable element.

Northwest of India, close to the Caspian Sea, there lived many centuries ago a group of wanderers who were of the same race as the Vedic Aryans. At some point during the second millenium B.C., one group of these Aryan invaders went to India (Hinduism developed in this group), and another entered present-day Armenia, Azarbaijan and the Iranian plateau. Zoroastrianism developed in the hard and arid soil of the Iranian plateau – an area that historians sometimes prefer to call ancient Persia.

As far as we know, the religion of ancient Persia was similar in many respects to the Vedic religion in India. Many of the gods worshipped in Persia were similar to the gods of India. Prominent among the deities were nature gods such as Sky: Vivahvant (the Vedic Vavasvant); Wind: Vayu (the Vedic Vayu); Sun: Mithra (the Vedic Mitra); Water: Haurvatat (the Vedic Sarvatat); Fire: Atar (the Vedic Agni), and so on.

Along with these gods there were innumerable good and evil spirits that were invoked and worshipped. Such were Death: Yima (the Vedic Yama); Truth: Asha (the Vedic Rta); Immortality: Ameretat (the Vedic Amrta), and the like.

The central ritual of the Iranian religion consisted of at least three forms of sacrifices: the animal sacrifice, the libation (drink) sacrifice, and the fire sacrifice. The animal and libation sacrifices seem to have been combined into one ritual, and the available evidence suggests this ritual was something of a drunken orgy. The traditional ritual consisted of slaughtering a bull or ox while the attending priests shouted and danced. During this ceremony, the priests also performed the libation rite in which they squeezed the juice from the *haoma* plant (in Vedic, the *soma* plant) and formally drank it, sometimes sharing the drink with worshippers. This juice must have been fermented and was certainly intoxicating, for, as we shall see later, the prophet Zoroaster condemned the priests for what he described as their filthy drunkenness and for their attempts to deceive the people.

The fire sacrifice of the ancient Persians is of particular interest, not only because of its similarity to the Vedic fire ceremony, but also because of its historical significance in Zoroastrianism: it remains the most important ritual in the religion to the present day. Although the details of the ancient ceremony are not too clear, it was generally a

Sandalwood for the sacred fire; but Zoroastrians are not fire-worshippers. Fire is only a symbol of Ahura Mazdah's greatness. Here, worshippers offer homage and prayers at home in front of an altar that includes the image of the prophet Zarathustra. (Courtesy of Illustrated Weekly of India)

ritual to consecrate the ground upon which the sacrificial fire was to be lit. Part of the consecration ritual consisted of sprinkling the ground with *haoma* juice, and then laying out the animal to be sacrificed. Worshippers who stood by had to cover their faces in adoration of the sacred fire.

The priests who performed the ceremonies and who claimed that they could control and influence the benevolent and malevolent spirits, came to be called *magi*. The method by which they practised their art was called *magic*. They not only claimed to influence divine powers in order to control everyday events, but were experts in the occult sciences. They interpreted dreams, received and delivered omens, foretold future events, read signs through the movements of stars or the flight of birds, and practised various kinds divination.

Such, then, were the religious practices in the Iranian plateau when the prophet Zarathustra (known to us through the Greeks as Zoroaster) appeared on the scene. His monotheistic tendency (his tendency to favour a belief in one god) and his teaching of ethical dualism (the struggle between good and evil), affected contemporary religious practices. The impact of Zoroaster was so forceful that the reformed religion which he left has ever since borne his name.

The Avesta

It is difficult to identify a historical figure who was known as Zoroaster. Indeed, there are some scholars who doubt that such a person ever lived and argue that he was simply a mythical figure created to account for a religious reform movement which developed in ancient Persia. Most scholars, however, through the careful study of the Zoroastrian scriptures (called the Avesta) have concluded that a man called Zoroaster did exist.

The Avesta, the sacred book, consists of ancient writings composed and written over a period of one thousand years – the earliest portion composed before the sixth century B.C. and the latest portion written around the fourth century A.D. According to tradition, the Avesta once consisted of a vast literature, but today only a small part survives.

Three principal groups of writings can be distinguished within the Avesta.

THE YASNA. This is a collection of prayer and liturgy formulae. Within this collection are a group of hymns, or songs, called the Gathas, which are believed to be hymns written by Zoroaster. The Gathas fill only seventeen chapters out of the seventy-two chapters of the Yasna. They are of special interest to scholars because scholars believe that these seventeen chapters are older than the writings in the rest of the Avesta and because they have found a close link between the language and history of the Gathas and the language and history of the Rig Vedas (the collection of sacred texts of ancient India and the oldest known documents in Sanskrit). This discovery seems to support the belief of many scholars that both writings have a common cultural and linguistic origin.

THE YASHT. This is a collection of sacrificial hymns addressed to individual deities.

THE VIDEVDAT. Less correctly known as the Vendidad, literally meaning "Law (*dat*) against (*vi*) the demons (*dev*)," this group of writings is concerned largely with ritual purification.

What is known about the date and authorship of the Gathas? Although the generally accepted view is that the Gathas represent the words of Zoroaster, the opinions of experts on the Avesta differ widely. Some think that Zoroaster composed and wrote the Gathas around the seventh or sixth century B.C.; others think that the Gathas were composed in the main by him, but that occasional verses were later added by his disciples. Still others suggest that the Gathas, although originally composed by the prophet Zoroaster, were preserved only in memory for centuries before they were written down. Whatever theory is held about their composition, the general view is that the Gathas are the only authentic documents concerning the life and teachings of the prophet Zoroaster.

Who, then, was Zoroaster? When and where was he born? What was his message and how did it affect the religion of ancient Persia?

Zoroaster

Most authorities accept the account in ancient Persian tradition, which holds that Zoroaster was born around the seventh century B.C. in the town of Azarbaijan, northwest of Media, close to the border of Armenia. His father Pourushaspa came from the family of the Spitamas, whose genealogy was traced back through forty-five generations to Gayomart, the first man (like Judaism's and Christianity's Adam) in ancient Persian mythology. His mother Drughdhova came from the well-to-do clan of the Hvogvas. It is said that at the age of fifteen Zoroaster's mother conceived by a heavenly shaft of light and gave virgin birth to the prophet.

The accounts of the prophet's birth, infancy and early life abound with miraculous events. One story tells that when Zoroaster was born, the earth trembled, a heavenly light shone around the house, and the universe thrilled with gladness as sounds of joy heralded the birth of the child, who astonished everyone by bursting into a triumphant laugh with his first breath. However, the demons and evil spirits did not passively accept this event, but made a number of attempts to kill him. They tried to choke him at the very moment of delivery, but at every attempt some miracle occurred to save him. While he was still in the cradle, Zoroaster would have been burned in the Fire-Temple, had not a miracle saved his life. In another incident, a herd of cows would surely have trampled the infant if the first cow had not stood over the young Zoroaster to protect him until the entire herd had passed by.

At the age of seven, Zoroaster was placed with a wise teacher for eight years to study the sciences and religious practices of the day. At the age of fifteen, he returned home to assume the rights of manhood. In this coming-of-age ceremony, still performed by Zoroastrian youth, young Zoroaster put on the "sacred shirt" and the "sacred girdle", symbols of his confirmation into the religion of his people. After this event, oddly enough, there are few traditional accounts which describe the fifteen years that elapsed before he received his enlightenment and his mission.

It seems that Zoroaster wandered away into the wilderness to meditate, and spent these fifteen years in a cave on a mountainside. Like Buddha, a century later in India, Zoroaster was deeply impressed by the problem of human suffering. Evil seemed to be everywhere. Raids, oppression, disease, famine, death – all darkened the lives of people. So Zoroaster wrestled with his own despair; and in one instance it seemed that an evil spirit was beside him to challenge him.

Zoroaster had spent fifteen years in fruitless meditation and had reached the age of thirty when enlightenment came. The story goes that as Zoroaster sat one evening in front of his cave watching the sunset, he suddenly leaped to his feet with joy. His struggles had ended, his inspiration had come, for in that moment he identified all the troubles and sufferings of the world with the sunset that divided day from night, light from darkness.

Just as a full day consists of a day and a night, of light and darkness, so the world consists of good and evil. Just as the day and night can never change their natural course, so good can never become evil, nor can evil ever become good. Just as the day must always be light and the night dark, so good must always be good and evil must always be evil. Hence, it was very clear to Zoroaster that the world was ruled by two Forces: one Good and the other Evil. The Good Force he called Ahura Mazdah (literally, "Wise Lord"), and the Evil Force he named Angra Mainyu ("Lie – Demon").

If good was always good, and evil was always evil, then the good spirits or gods could never do evil, nor could the evil spirits or gods do good. "I will go and tell my people," determined Zoroaster, "that their gods of fear and superstition are only agents of Angra Mainyu, and that the time is coming when Ahura Mazdah, the supreme God of light and truth, will vanquish Angra Mainyu."

At dawn the following day, Zoroaster was standing peacefully by the sacred river Daiti, when he suddenly saw Ahura Mazdah in a wonderful vision. One is reminded of the prophetic visions in other religions, like Isaiah's vision as told in the Judiac tradition, or the Christian story of the vision that came to John on the isle of Patmos, while he was writing

During the special festival of *Ava* (in April), Zoroastrians of India, known as Parsees, gather by the seaside (or river, lake, pond) at dawn to offer homage to the sacred element of water. Coconuts, sugar, and flowers are offered during meditation and prayers. Both men and women cover their heads during any act of worship or ceremony. (Courtesy of Illustrated Weekly of India)

the book of Revelation. It is difficult to determine just what took place in the mystical experience of Zoroaster, since later tradition, recognizing the importance of this theophany (vision of God), embellished it with elaborate details. The central fact in the experience, however, was that Zoroaster was led by an archangel into the presence of Ahura Mazdah, where he was taught the cardinal principles of true religion. Zoroastrian calendars start from this great event, fixed at May 5, 630 B.C., and call it the first Year of the Religion (1 A.R.).

From Zoroaster's intense perception at sunset and his vision on the following day, came his religious belief in the dualism of the universe, in the two forces constantly struggling with each other. The outcome of this long struggle, Zoroaster believed, would be the ultimate triumph of Ahura Mazdah, the Lord of good, truth, wisdom and light, over Angra Mainyu, the Lord of evil, falsehood, ignorance and darkness.

After he embarked on his mission of preaching, it took Zoroaster ten years to win some converts: the king and court of Bactria. These particular converts gave a great boost to his efforts since his religion now had royal assent. His organized campaigns for propagating the new faith led him then as far as China. Zoroaster died at the age of seventy-seven. Though he had three wives and a number of sons and daughters, he is thought to have been a solitary wanderer most of his life. The teachings he left behind were to mark him as one of the world's great and influential prophets.

Ahura Mazdah

What were Zoroaster's teachings? In what way did his message differ from traditional beliefs and customs? Zoroaster was repelled by what he considered to be the religious corruption of his day and was deeply offended by the base practices of the false prophets, who not only distorted the sacred scriptures, but through their evil doctrines diverted men from the best course of action and the divine purpose in life. Zoroaster had no doubt that such men were "followers of the Lie" and he openly condemned them as the "beloved of the Daevas (Demons or Evil Spirits), and obstructors of the Good Mind", enemies of the divine purpose of Ahura Mazdah and of his law. Zoroaster knew very well that these condemnations would bring him into sharp conflict with the sacrificial priests of the Daevas; yet in the face of persecution, he spoke courageously against the priests, calling them "wilfully blind" and "wilfully deaf" men who hindered the "cultivation, peace and perfection of Creation through their own deeds and doctrines". In spite of opposition Zoroaster sounded the death knell of the drunken *haoma* ritual.

Zoroaster did not, however, abolish all elements of the ancient religion. Long before Zoroaster, the ancient Persians had revered and worshipped Atar (god of fire). Zoroaster seems to have shifted the emphasis. Ahura Mazdah, he said, was like Atar, in that fire is light, and light is the symbol of Ahura Mazdah. Atar remained a part of the Zoroastrian scheme as the symbol of Ahura Mazdah's light and righteousness. Zoroastrians have ever since paid a perpetual tribute to this symbolic element.

Zoroastrian
Symbol of God
Ahura Mazdah

Among the collection of deities that the ancient Persians recognized, some benevolent, others malevolent, Zoroaster maintained that his God Ahura Mazdah was supreme. Ahura Mazdah, the "Lord of Life and Wisdom", was the "First and also the Last of all eternity". He was the Mighty and Holy, the Creator of all, giver of all good, and the giver of life. To those who looked up to Ahura Mazdah with awe, he was a "friend, brother, nay father". Because his God was "Holy, Eternal, Just, Omniscient (All-knowing), the Primeval Being, Creator of all and the origin of all goodness", Zoroaster chose Ahura Mazdah "alone as master". This choice is evidence of Zoroaster's tendency towards monotheism. Thus Zoroaster tried to reform the polytheistic religion of his time by gathering together the various symbolic representations of struggle which lay scattered in the ancient myths of gods, spirits, demons and monsters, and welding them into a single, universal conflict: good versus evil.

Freedom of Choice

Zoroaster saw mankind as divided into two opposing parties: the *asha-vants* (followers of truth), who were the just and the god-fearing; and the *dregvants* (followers of evil and falsehood), among whom were classed "evil rulers, evil doers, evil speakers, those of evil conscience, and evil thinkers". The basic dualism that the prophet saw here and now on earth, he projected to the whole cosmos. He believed that this fundamental tension existed in all spheres, the material, the spiritual, and the cosmic. Against a transcendental "good mind" stood the "evil mind"; against the "good spirit" stood the "evil spirit"; and so on. And in every sphere, among every pair of opposites, man has to make a choice. Every man must ultimately make his own choice for good or for evil. Zoroaster's insistence on man's *freedom of choice* is a marked characteristic of the Gathas. Thus, what stands out in Zoroaster's teaching is not only the ethical dualism of good versus evil but the importance of man as an arbiter between them.

> . . . O Ahura Mazdah,
> From the beginning Thou didst create for us, through Thy
> mind, physical bodies, consciences and wills;
> . . . Thou didst infuse the soul of life into mortal bones;
> . . . Thou didst grant us capacities to act and words to guide,
> so that man may choose freely . . .
>
> Yasna 31.11

Zoroaster reduced the whole human drama, the ultimate purpose of human existence, to one essential element: *choice*. However, although man is free to pursue either of the two paths – good or evil – his choice here and now determines his eternal destiny.

> Hear that which is the highest good!
> With an enlightened mind,
> Look upon the two sides between which each man must choose
> for himself!
> Awake! . . . before the great and final consummation is upon
> you!
>
> So understand, O mortal men,
> The decrees which Mazdah has ordained
> Regarding happiness and suffering!
>
> Long period of suffering for the wicked,
> And rewards for the righteous!
>
> Then, eternal joy shall reign everywhere!
>
> Yasna 30.2, 11

Human choices were made, according to Zoroaster, in the three areas of thought, word, and deed: a "human triad". Hence, man's choice was not restricted to his actions only, nor to his words only, but encompassed all three areas of human capacity. Life was a matter of choice between good thoughts, good words, good deeds and evil thoughts, evil words, evil deeds.

To Zoroaster, the universe was a scene of constant battle between a pair of coexistent, divine Forces or Powers: one, Ahura Mazdah (later called Ormazd), represented light, truth and life; the other, Angra Mainyu (later called Ahriman), represented darkness, falsehood, and absence of life. Ahura Mazdah was incapable of creating evil. Wisdom, justice, truth, love and all ideal human endeavours came from Ahura Mazdah. On the other hand, the originator and initiator of all evil, pain, suffering, disease and death was Angra Mainyu.

This brings us to the question of the origin of the universe and human beings. Who created man and the universe? Angra Mainyu or Ahura Mazdah? According to Zoroaster, the creator was

> He [Ahura Mazdah] who, through His holy mind thought: "Let the blessed expanses be filled with light."
>
> He Himself [Ahura Mazdah], in His wisdom . . . created . . . physical bodies, consciences and wills . . .
>
> Yasna 31.7-11

Ahura Mazdah then is the creator of all. But because the very essence of Ahura Mazdah is freedom of choice, he also grants to every individual the capacity to choose; so that all those who believe in him and even those who disbelieve in him or are ignorant of him share at least this characteristic in common – they have the capacity to decide whether they wish good or evil. Without interfering in any way with this quality of choice, Ahura Mazdah desires that his creatures come to him of their own free will.

But what, finally, is to be the outcome of the long struggle between Ahura Mazdah and Angra Mainyu? Will Angra Mainyu forever afflict man and the universe? Will Ahura Mazdah and Angra Mainyu eternally oppose each other?

Whatever doubts later Zoroastrians may have had on this point, Zoroaster felt certain that Ahura Mazdah would eventually triumph. Good would overcome evil. A general ressurection was to take place at the end of life in this world, and each soul was to be subjected to an ordeal of fire and molten metal. To the followers of Ahura Mazdah, this ordeal would seem like passing through warm milk, but to the followers of Angra Mainyu, it would be a terrible burning. The Gathas do not clearly spell out whether the forces and adherents of evil, including Angra Mainyu, would be entirely consumed by the fiery ordeal, or would be hurled into the "abode of lies" (hell?). Whatever their fate, evil would be completely abolished, and eternal bliss would reign everywhere.

Later amplification of Zoroaster's teaching vividly portrays the process of individual judgement. Each soul was to be judged after death at the "Separator Bridge" which spans the abyss of hell, and leads to Paradise at the other end. While the soul crosses the Bridge, the records of that soul's life on earth are opened and read. If good thoughts, words and deeds outweigh evil thoughts, words and deeds, then the soul crosses without difficulty to Paradise. But if the reverse is the case, then the soul is unable to go beyond the centre of the Bridge, but automatically falls to its doom. While Paradise is described as the "best existence, the abode of the good, where the sun shines forever and the righteous enjoy eternal bliss", hell is described as the "worst existence, the ill-smelling region, where there is continual darkness, and where suffering voices cry out sadly forever in loneliness".

Later Developments

Just as modifications eventually creep into every religion, so in time the religious tradition established by Zoroaster changed. The old gods reappeared and new ones were introduced. In fact, even Zoroaster himself came to be considered a god.

Furthermore, Zoroaster's concept of the dualism between Ahura Mazdah and Angra Mainyu created an important problem in later Zoroastrian theology. If Ahura Mazdah was eventually to triumph, and hence be more powerful than Angra Mainyu, then it seemed that Angra Mainyu and all evil must exist by permission of Ahura Mazda. If, on the other hand, Angra Mainyu was an eternal principle, then Ahura Mazdah could not be regarded as the sole creator. Disputes on such questions as these led in time to the formation of many movements and groups within the religion, among which were Mazdaeism, Zurvanism and Mithraism.

Before the Christian era, Mithraism penetrated the Roman Empire from the Near East, and during the second and third centuries A.D. it became the strongest religious rival of Christianity. Christianity had many startling similarities to Mithraism. Followers of Mithra regarded the seventh day of each week (Sunday, and not Saturday) as a sacred day to the Sun God Mithra. The birth of Mithra was celebrated toward the end of December, more or less simultaneously with the winter solstice which falls on the shortest day in the northern hemisphere.

Worshippers of Mithra had a ritual similar to the Eucharist (Communion) ceremony in the Christian community, in which they took consecrated bread and wine, and a bell tolled at the climax of their service.

Moreover, the theological concepts of Mithraism and Christianity have much in common. All souls after death are to appear before the Judgement seat of Mithra (or of God in Christianity), where the good are rewarded with eternal Paradise and the wicked are punished in eternal damnation by the forces of Ahriman (or of Satan in Christianity). These and other similarities between the two religions not only made Mithraism a rival to Christianity, but caused a certain amount of confusion. Ultimately Christianity supplanted Mithraism and various other religions by combining in itself many of the values and functions of its competing religions.

An interesting footnote to Zoroastrianism is the history of the *magi*. The *magi* are thought to have originated not as a group or sect, but as a tribe (perhaps from Media) which embraced Zoroaster's religion and later supplied its priests. They were widely known for their skill in the magical arts, divination and astrology. They became more and more influential, until finally they were recognized as the expert exponents

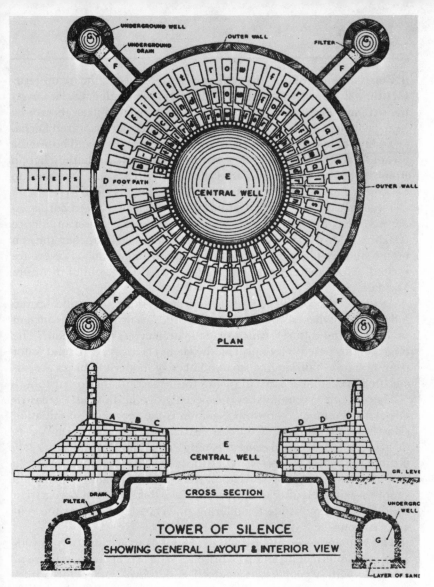

PLAN

CROSS SECTION

TOWER OF SILENCE
SHOWING GENERAL LAYOUT & INTERIOR VIEW

According to Zoroastrianism, it is a sin to defile any of the elements. Therefore, the dead body cannot be cremated, immersed in water, or buried under the earth. The circular platform inside the Tower of Silence is well cemented and consists of three rows of stone slabs. Row A is for males, B for females, and C for children. The path marked D is for corpse-bearers. After the funeral rites, the body is placed in the tower and the vultures set in. The bones dry and slip into the central well (E) where they mix with lime and phosphorus and disintegrate. The holes in the inner side of the well lead the rainwater into four underground drains (F) which lead into four underground wells (G), the bottoms of which are covered with a thick layer of sand. A mixture of charcoal and sandstone, renewed from time to time, is placed at the end of each drain to purify the rainwater that flows over the bones. Prayers continue for three days after the disposal of the body. (Courtesy of Illustrated Weekly of India) of Zoroastrianism. The story of their visit to Mary and the infant Jesus (Matthew 2:1-2) is in itself proof of their fame and influence. However, their tremendous power and the Zoroastrian religion itself received a near-fatal blow in A.D. 651, when the Islamic invaders captured Persia.

Today there are very few Zoroastrians left in Persia. Those who escaped the Islamic conquest settled in India; presently they live in Bombay and its vicinity and are called *Parsees* (Persians). No one can become a Zoroastrian or Parsee who is not one by birth.

Two kinds of buildings are important elements of modern Zoroastrianism: one is the Fire-Temple and the other is the Tower of Silence (Dakhma). Most Parsees visit the Fire-Temple at least four times a month, though many devout followers attend almost daily. Prayers are recited before the eternal flame of the sacred fire, symbol of Ahura Mazdah.

At the Tower of Silence, usually located on a remote and barren hilltop, the bodies of the dead are exposed, according to the ancient practice, to the vultures, which strip the flesh in less than an hour. The object of this practice is to protect the elements of fire, earth and water from pollution. Although a small number of modern thinkers are advocating cremation, many still cling to the sacred, ancient custom.

There is one ceremony that is especially significant to all Zoroastrians. This ceremony, known as Naojote, is the ceremony of initiation of a child into the fold of the Zoroastrian religion. The term *Naojote* is made up of two words: *nao*, meaning "new", and *jote*, or rather *zote*, meaning "to offer prayers". Hence the word Naojote would mean, "a new initiate to offer (Zoroastrian) prayers". The ceremony is so named simply because it is after the performance of this rite that a Zoroastrian child is held responsible for offering prayers and observing the religous customs.

The Naojote ceremony (which corresponds to Bar-mitzvah in Judaism and Confirmation among Christians) consists of the investiture of the child with a *sudrah* (sacred shirt) and a *kusti* (sacred thread). A Zoroastrian may dress as he likes, but ideally he must wear the sudrah and the kusti as the sign and symbol of his religion.

A child is initiated into the Zoroastrian faith at the age of seven in India, or nine in Iran (Persia), except in the event of unavoidable circumstances, in which case the ceremony may be postponed to any time up to the age of fifteen, at which time the investiture must take place.

> It is incumbent on all those of the good religion, men and women, every one who attains to fifteen years to wear the

The Naojote ceremony, which signifies new life, initiates a boy or a girl into the Zoroastrian fold. For the first time the initiate is made to wear a *sudrah* and a *kusti*. (Courtesy of Illustrated Weekly of India)

> sacred thread girdle, because the sacred thread girdle is to be
> a girding of the loins and to preserve obedience to the Lord.
>
> Saddar 10.1

Prior to the investiture a child is given a ceremonial bath in sacred or holy water by the officiating priests. Then follows the recital of a prayer by the priest and the child, after which the following Declaration of Faith is spoken by the child:

> Praised be the most righteous, the wisest, the most holy and
> the best Mazdaean Law which is the gift of Mazdah. The good,
> true, and perfect religion, which God has sent to this world,
> is that which Prophet Zoroaster has brought. That religion is
> the religion of Zoroaster, the religion of Ahura Mazdah communicated to holy Zoroaster.

After this declaration, the rite of investiture with the sudrah and kusti is performed by the priest. Then follows the recital of the Articles of Faith, spoken by the child and priest in unison:

> O Almighty! Come to my help.
> I am a worshipper of God.
> I am a Zoroastrian worshipper of God.
> I agree to praise the Zoroastrian religion and to believe in
> that religion.

I praise good thoughts, good words, and good deeds.

I praise the good Mazdaean religion, which curtails discussions and quarrels, which brings about kinship or brotherhood, which is holy, which, of all the religions that have yet flourished and are likely to flourish in the future, is the greatest, the best and the most excellent, and which is the religion given by God to Zoroaster.

I believe that all good things proceed from God.

May the Mazdaean religion be thus praised.

The Naojote ceremony ends with the recital of a benediction by the officiating priest. Nevertheless, the most significant part is the recitation of the Articles of Faith by which the initiate conforms his belief in the efficacy of his own good thoughts, good words, and good deeds. The Zoroastrian looks to no one but himself for the salvation of his soul. The whole structure of the Zoroastrian religion rests on this moral triad: purity of thoughts, words, and deeds.

This outline of Zoroastrianism has done little more than suggest its incalculable influence on other religions, especially Judaism, Christianity and Islam. The ideas of the "devil", "satan", the "adversary", and the vivid imagery of heaven and hell all stem from Zoroaster and the seventh century B.C. Moreover, down through the ages, the indirect but powerful contribution of Zoroastrian ideas has been seen in a number of literary classics: Dante's *Divine Comedy*, Adamnan's *Vision of Heaven and Hell*, and Milton's *Paradise Lost*. In a brief study such as this, however, it is impossible to give an accurate idea of the pervasive influence that Zoroaster and his ideas have had in shaping the patterns of modern world religions.

Wedding ceremonies are performed in the bride's house and solemnized by two or more priests in the presence of witnesses from both families. Rice and bits of coconuts (probably borrowed from Hindu customs) are showered on the couple. (Courtesy of Illustrated Weekly of India)

Glossary

The purpose of the glossary is to explain briefly but accurately the numerous terms used in this book, and to help the reader to associate each term with the appropriate religion. The following abbreviations are used:

Jud. Judaism   Chr. Christianity
Isl. Islam   Hin. Hinduism
Bud. Buddhism   Zor. Zoroastrianism

Abhidhamma (Bud.) See *Tripitaka.*

Agni (Hin.) Deity identified with fire.

Agnostic A person who claims that no-one can know whether there is a God or a spiritual world.

Ahura Mazdah (Zor.) The Zoroastrian God of Life and Wisdom.

Al-Jihad (Isl.) See *Jihad.*

Allah (Isl.) The Islamic, all-powerful God.

Ameretat (Zor.) Immortality; the sixth of the six Zoroastrian Divine Powers.

Amida (Bud.) See *Amitabha.*

Amitabha (Bud.) One of the Bodhisattvas regarded as the incarnation of Infinite Compassion and the object of worship in the Pure Land Schools. The Chinese term is O-mi-to, while the Japanese term is Amida.

Anatta (Bud.) Non-ego. The essential Buddhist doctrine which affirms that there is no permanent self, or ego, or soul, which makes the individual or person. It represents one of the three characteristics of existence; the others are dukkha and anicca.

Angra Mainyu (Zor.) The Lie-Demon or Evil Force who opposes Ahura Mazdah.

Anicca (Bud.) Impermanence; one of the three characteristics of existence; the others are dukkha and anatta.

Apocrypha (Chr.) The "hidden" books; a collection of about fourteen disputed books appended between the Old and New Testaments.

Aranyaka (Hin.) Relating to a forest. Name of a part of the Vedas included in the Brahmana section.

Arhat (Bud.) In Theravada Buddhism, the ideal person who has completed the discipline required to attain liberation. (See *Bodhisattva* for ideal Mahayanist.)

Asha (Zor.) Truth, Order, Righteousness; the first of six Zoroastrian Divine Powers.

Ashavant (Zor.) A follower of Asha, or Truth; always contrasted with Dregvant.

Ashrama (Hin.) Any of the "stages" in the life of a Brahmin, of which there are four: student, householder, forest-dweller, and beggar (sannyasin).

Atar (Zor.) Fire. Refers also to the Flaming Fire of Thought.

Atharva-Veda (Hin.) See *Vedas*.

Atheist A person who believes that there is no God.

Atman (Hin.) The individual "self", "soul", "essence", or "nature of man". Written with a capital "A", it refers to the Supreme Soul.

Avesta (Zor.) The Zoroastrian sacred scripture, which comprises three principal groups:

The Yasna: A collection of hymns, prayers and liturgy, including the Gathas (songs) ascribed to Zoroaster.

The Yasht: A collection of sacrificial hymns addressed to deities.

The Videvdat: A collection of purification rituals.

Bhagavad Gita (Hin.) A portion within the Hindu epic of the Mahabharata used as a devotional book.

Bhakti Marga (Hin.) See *Marga*.

Bible (Jud.) A collection of twenty-four writings grouped into three main sections:

Torah (The Law): consisting of five books

Nebhi'im (The Prophets): consisting of eight books

Kethubim (The Writings): consisting of eleven books.

(Chr.) A collection of sixty-six writings grouped into two main sections:
Old Testament: the same twenty-four books as the scriptures of Judaism, but grouped differently so that the number consists of thirty-nine books

New Testament: a collection of twenty-seven books written between A.D. 50 and 100.

Bodhi (Bud.) Enlightenment.

Bodhisattva (Bud.) In Mahayana Buddhism an individual who has attained englightenment, but moved by compassion to aid humanity, postpones his own entrance into nirvana; regarded as a "saviour".

Brahma (Hin.) The God from whom all things emanate; the first person of the Hindu Trinity; the other two are Vishnu and Siva. (See also *Hindu Triad*)

Brahman (Hin.) The non-dual, self-existent Divine Essence; the Supreme Soul or Source, from Whom all things emanate, by Whom they are preserved, and to Whom they return; the Absolute Reality. Not an object of worship, but rather of meditation and knowledge.

Brahmana (Hin.) A portion of the Vedas which contains rules for various sacrificial rites; also contains explanatory remarks.

Buddha (Bud.) Not the name of a person, but a title meaning "Enlightened One", or "Illumined One". There have been past Buddhas and there will be others in the future. The historical figure Siddhartha Gautama is one of the Buddhas, though he is often referred to as The Buddha.

Caliph (Isl.) Successor; a title given to the successors of Mohammed.

Canon The name given by religious authorities to a group of writings accepted as scriptures, or of divine authority.

Ch'an (Bud.) A Chinese term meaning "meditation". Introduced by Bodhidharma in the sixth century A.D. the Ch'an sect developed into a school that emphasizes meditation as a means of liberation.

Chandala (Hin.) An "outcast" in the Hindu society; an offspring of a Sudra father and a Brahmin mother.

Christos (Chr.) A Greek word meaning "Anointed One"; used as a title (Christ) for the historical Jesus.

Daevas (Zor.) Demons, evil spirits or deities.

Dalai-Lama (Bud.) The spiritual and temporal Head (Pope) of Tibet.

Dhamma (Hin.) Duty; obligation; right; justice; religion.

(Bud.) The Truth; The Way; The Law; Reality.

Dhammapada (Bud.) The "Way" or "Law" of the Buddha's Teaching; a collection of 423 verses found in the Sutta-Pitaka section of the Tripitaka.

Dharma Same as *Dhamma*.

Doctrine Principle of belief; in the religious realm, an essential view or concept.

Dregvant (Zor.) Followers of the Drug — Evil, Lie. Zoroaster divided mankind into two categories, the Ashavants and the Dregvants.

Dukkha (Bud.) Pain, sorrow, suffering, unhappiness; the first of the Four Noble Truths and one of the three characteristics of existence; the other two are anatta and anicca.

Duraosha (Zor.) Death-dispelling; an epithet applied by Zoroaster to the Haoma cult.

Emanate To issue from; to proceed from; to originate or arise from.

Essene (Jud.) An important Jewish community which flourished in Palestine during the lifetime of Jesus. The collection of their written materials discovered in 1947 is known as the Dead Sea Scrolls.

Eucharist (Chr.) Holy Communion; the Lord's Supper. One of the sacraments performed by all Christian churches.

Gemarah (Jud.) The collection of discussions relative to the Mishnah, necessitated by the change of language from Hebrew to Aramaic.

Guru (Hin.) A spiritual teacher who instructs from the scriptures and conducts the necessary ceremonies in connection with his investiture.

Hadith (Isl.) The collection of "Traditions", especially the sayings and actions of the prophet Mohammed.

Haggadah (Jud.) The collection of legendary, theological, and non-legal materials in the Midrash.

Hajj (Isl.) Pilgrimage to the sacred Ka'aba in Mecca, which every Muslim is obliged to make at least once in a lifetime.

Halakah (Jud.) A collection of legal materials in the Midrash.

Hannukah (Jud.) The term means "consecration" or "dedication" The Feast of Rededication celebrated annually around December 25, commemorating the Maccabean cleansing of the Temple in 165 B.C. from the "pollution" of Hellenistic worship.

Haoma (Zor.) Sacred plant whose juice is used in Zoroastrian ritual.

Haptanhaiti (Zor.) A collection of seven chapters in the Avesta.

Haurvatat (Zor.) Perfection; the fifth of the six Zoroastrian Divine Powers.

Hegira (Isl.) Flight; in A.D. 622, the flight of Mohammed and his disciples from Mecca to Medina on September 24. All Muslim calendars are dated from this year.

Hinayana (Bud.) A term meaning "Lesser" or "Smaller Vehicle", coined by the Mahayanists to distinguish it from their own school. Also called Theravada or Southern School; mainly concentrated in Ceylon, Burma, Thailand and Cambodia. One of the two major divisions in Buddhism; the other is Mahayana.

Hindu Triad (Hin.) The Hindu Trinity or Triad is called "Trimurti" and is considered to be the three manifestations of Brahman:
Brahma: the God of Creation
Vishnu: the God of Preservation
Shiva: the God of Destruction

Iblis Distortion of the Greek word *diabolos*, meaning Devil or Satan.

Indra (Hin.) Deity identified with Strength: sky, atmosphere, rain, thunderbolt.

Injil (Isl.) An Arabic term meaning "Evangel", "Gospel".

Inquisition An ecclesiastical (church-associated) tribunal, sometimes referred to as "the Holy Office", established by the Roman Catholic Church in the Middle Ages for the trial and punishment of heretics.

Islam (Isl.) An Arabic term meaning "submission". The name of the religion founded by the prophet Mohammed.

Jataka (Bud.) A Pali term meaning "birth story". A collection of 550 stories, found in the Sutta-Pitaka section of the Tripitaka, about the former existences of The Buddha.

Jihad (Isl.) Holy War.

Jinn (Isl.) Rebellious angels.

Jnana Marga (Hin.) See *Marga*.

Jodo (Bud.) The Japanese school of the Pure Land Sect.

Ka'aba (Isl.) The rectangular or cube-like shrine at Mecca; the centre of Islamic pilgrimage.

Karma (Hin. & Bud.) The term means "action" and refers to the moral law of cause and effect in which a man "reaps what he sows".

Karma Marga (Hin.) See *Marga*.

Kashruth (Jud.) Specified dietary law which forms an integral part of the Judaic religious life.

Kethubhim (Jud.) The Writings; the third group of eleven books in the Judaic sacred scripture. (See also *Bible*)

Koan (Bud.) A technical term used in Zen Buddhism; a riddle, a phrase, or a word of nonsensical language which cannot be solved by reason or by the intellect; used as an exercise for breaking the limitations of reason and thought; develops a higher faculty of intuition.

Kshatriya (Hin.) The second caste in the Hindu society; a member of the military or governing order.

Kusti (Zor.) A sacred thread given at the time of initiation.

Lama (Bud.) A term or title used for some members of the Tibetan Order of Buddhism.

Mahabharata (Hin.) The longer of the two great epics, within which is the Bhagavad Gita. The other epic is the Ramayana.

Mahayana (Bud.) The school of the "Great Vehicle"; one of the two major divisions in Buddhism, the other being Theravada or Hinayana; mainly concentrated in China, Tibet, Korea, Japan, Mongolia, and Viet Nam.

Maitreya (Bud.) The name of the Bodhisattva who will be the future Buddha.

Mandala (Bud.) Symbolic diagram, chart or circle, used especially as an aid for mystical and magical rites in Buddhist esoteric schools. (See also *Mantra* and *Mudra*)

Mantra (Bud.) A magical formula based on the power of sound; used especially in Buddhist esoteric schools. (See also *Mandala* and *Mudra*)

Manu (Hin.) The Laws or Code of Manu is considered a sacred book in Hinduism. It includes various duties, regulations, laws and ethical issues.

Mara (Bud.) The Tempter, or Devil; the personification of evil in Buddhist mythology.

Marga (Hin.) The word *marga* means "way" or "path". There are three major Paths of liberation:
Karma Marga: The Path of Works
Jnana Marga: The Path of Knowledge
Bhakti Marga: The Path of Devotion

Mazzebah (Jud.) Stone pillar.

Messiah (Jud. & Chr.) A Hebrew term meaning "Anointed One". In Judaism, a figure expected to appear; referred to as Jesus by Christians.

Midrash (Jud.) The term means "to search out" or "to investigate". The collection of literary works containing scriptural expositions and interpretations of either a legal (halakah) or non-legal (haggadah) character.

Minaret (Isl.) A tower attached to the Islamic Mosque, from the top of which a muezzin calls people to prayer.

Mishnah (Jud.) The term means "to repeat", or "to study", or "to teach". The collection of traditional writings concerning the Torah as assembled by Rabbi Judah ha-Nasi.

Mitra (Hin.) Deity identified with the Sun.

Mitzvah (Jud.) The performance of a religious act.

Moksha (Hin.) Liberation; release from the cycle of existences.

Mosque (Isl.) The Muslim place or building for prayer.

Mudra (Bud.) Ritual gesture of the hands and fingers used symbolically and magically, especially in the Buddhist esoteric schools. (See also *Mantra* and *Mandala*).

Muezzin (Isl.) A "crier"; one who "calls" people to prayer.

Muslim (Isl.) An Arabic term meaning "one who submits"; the name applies to followers of the Islamic religion. ·

Nebhi'im (Jud.) The Prophets. The second group of eight books in the sacred scripture of Judaism. (See also *Bible)*

New Testament (Chr.) See *Bible*.

Nirvana (Bud.) The term is derived from a word which means "extinguished through lack of fuel". The state achieved by the conquest of desire or craving; the supreme goal of Buddhist endeavour, which releases the individual from the cycle of existence.

Old Testament (Chr.) See *Bible*.

O-mi-to (Bud.) See *Amitabha*.

Parsee (Zor.) Name given to followers of Zoroastrianism.

Patriarch (Jud.) The name applied to the father or ruler of a family or tribe. (Chr.) The highest dignitary or head of the Eastern Orthodox Church.

Pentecost See *Shabuoth*.

Pesach (Jud.) The Passover Feast; celebrated annually since the second century A.D. during Easter (March-April) in commemoration of Israel's deliverance from Egypt (the Exodus).

Pharisees (Jud.) An influential religio-political party that arose probably during the second century B.C. Its main characteristic was its legalistic rigor, which eventually became a living influential movement in the mainstream of Judaism. There was constant tension and opposition between the Pharisees (the lay element in Judaism) and the Sadducees.

Pinda (Hin.) Little balls of rice pressed into a firm cake and used as an offering to ancestral spirits.

Pitaka (Bud.) A basket. See *Tripitaka*.

Pope (Chr.) The head of the Roman Catholic Church.

Prakriti (Hin.) Primordial matter. In the Sankhya system, the essential Oneness of man and the universe is divided into pairs of opposites, one pair being "Prakriti", and the other "Purusha" or Self.

Proselyte A convert to some group, party, or religion.

Purim (Jud.) An annual festival currently celebrated during the twelfth month of the Jewish calendar (Feb.-Mar.) in remembrance of the Jewish deliverance by Esther and Mordecai from Haman's scheme of destroying the Jews in the Persian empire.

Purusha (Hin.) The word means "self".

Qoheleth (Jud.) The Hebrew title for the book of Ecclesiastes.

Quraish (Isl.) An Arabian tribe which acted as the custodians of the Ka'aba shrine in Mecca; Mohammed belonged to the Quraish tribe.

Qur'an (Isl.) The term means "recitation", and is the name given to the Islamic sacred scripture.

Rajah (Hin.) Indian term for a prince, chieftain, or tribal head.

Ramadan (Isl.) The Muslim rite of fasting during the ninth month in the lunar calendar, commemorating the revelation that came to Mohammed.

Ramayana (Hin.) The shorter of the two Hindu epics. The other is the Mahabharata.

Rig-Veda (Hin.) See *Vedas.*

Rishi (Hin.) Indian term for a "holy sage" or "seer".

Rosh Hashanah (Jud.) The Jewish New Year; according to variations in the calendar, it falls around September – October.

Sabbath (Jud.) The seventh day of the week (Saturday), regarded as a Holy Day.

Sadducee (Jud.) The aristocratic priestly party in Judaism whose interests were centred in the Temple, and whose concepts and practices opposed those of the Pharisees. Probably arose after the Maccabean revolt in the second century B.C.

Sakya (Bud.) The name of the tribe or clan to which Siddhartha Gautama belonged.

Salat (Isl.) Prayer.

Sama-Veda (Hin.) See *Vedas.*

Samsara (Hin. & Bud.) The cycle of successive existences, or rebirths.

Sanatana Dharma (Hin.) The name given to the Hindu religion, meaning "Eternal Religion".

Sangha (Bud.) An assembly; the name given to the monastic order founded by Buddha.

Sankhya (Hin.) One of the six systems of philosophy; this one suggests a practical discipline of Jnana Marga in order to free the soul from all "evil matter" which binds one to the cycle of existence.

Satori (Bud.) Enlightenment; a technical term to describe a state of consciousness beyond the realm of differentiation.

Shabuoth (Jud.) An ancient agricultural feast called the Feast of the Weeks because it is celebrated 50 days, or "a week of weeks", after the first day of Passover. It also commemorates the day when Moses received the Ten Commandments.

(Chr.) Christians celebrate Pentecost (meaning "fiftieth day" in Greek) seven weeks after Easter Sunday.

Shahadah (Isl.) The Creed or Recitation: "There is no God but Allah, and Mohammed is his prophet."

Shaitan (Isl.) Satan.

Shekinah (Jud.) Divine presence; God's presence.

Shi'ite (Isl.) One of the main and "liberal" divisions in Islam; the other is the Sunni.

Shiva (Hin.) The third god in the Hindu Triad. (See also *Hindu Triad*)

Shraddha (Hin.) A domestic religious ritual consisting of periodic offerings of pinda to ancestral spirits.

Skandhas (Bud.) The five impermanent elements which form a person. These five elements are material qualities, perception, feelings, subconscious predispositions, and awareness.

Smriti (Hin.) The term means "what is remembered", and refers to the whole body of sacred tradition as distinguished from sruti, or revelation.

Sruti (Hin.) The sacred Vedic knowledge revealed to the rishis, and transmitted orally by Brahmins from generation to generation.

Sudra (Hin.) A person of the fourth (lowest) caste in the Hindu society, whose only duty, according to the Code of Manu, is to serve the three upper castes.

Sudrah (Zor.) A sacred shirt worn from the time of initiation.

Sukhavati (Bud.) The "Western Paradise" of the Pure Land sect, brought into existence by O-mi-to, or Amitabha.

Sukkoth (Jud.) The Feast of Tabernacles celebrated annually as a "Thanksgiving" festival.

Sunni (Isl.) One of the major and "orthodox" branches in Islam.

Sura (Isl.) Chapter.

Sutta (Bud.) See *Tripitaka*.

Synagogue (Jud.) The Jewish place or building of worship.

Tad ekam (Hin.) That One; the mysterious First Principle which is indescribable, uncharacterizable, and without qualities or attributes.

Talmud (Jud.) The comprehensive designation for the Mishna and the Gemarah, being a collection of commentaries, expositions, traditions, and precedents. There are two Talmuds:
Babylonian: recordings of the discussions of the scholars who lived in Babylon
Palestinian: recordings of the discussions of the scholars who lived in Palestine.

Tanha (Bud.) Selfish craving for sentient existence; the second of the Four Noble Truths.

Tathagata (Bud.) A title of the Buddha, used by himself and later by his followers. The derivation of the term is disputed.

Tat tvam asi (Hin.) An expression, or formula, which means "That art thou". Refers to man and the universe as being part of and one with the Absolute.

Tawreh (Isl.) Distortion of the Hebrew word "Torah".

Theist A person who believes that there is a God (or Gods) and a spiritual world.

Theravada (Bud.) The "Way of the Elders" School. This term is more favourable and acceptable than Hinayana. Theravada and Mahayana are the two main divisions in Buddhism. (See also *Hinayana*)

Torah (Jud.) The Law; the first of the three divisions in the sacred scriptures of Judaism. (See also *Bible*)

Tripitaka (Bud.) The term means "three baskets". Refers to the Pali Canon as accepted by the Theravada schools, and is divided into three main sections:
Vinaya-Pitaka: contains rules for the Sangha
Sutta-Pitaka: contains the sermons of the Buddha, and other collections
Abhidhamma-Pitaka: contains a collection of writings on mind-

development.

Tusika (Bud.) The fourth heaven-realm of the six, in which the Buddha exists while the Buddha-to-be, Maitreya, awaits his coming.

Upanishads (Hin.) A class of philosophical treatises (108 in number) attached to the Brahmana portion of the Vedas. Their purpose is the exposition of Vedic philosophy, and they are regarded as the basic source for "orthodox" Hindu schools of philosophy.

Vaisya (Hin.) A member of the third caste in the Hindu society, whose occupation is trade, agriculture, or cattle-rearing.

Varuna (Hin.) One of the oldest Vedic gods, described as Creator of Heaven and Earth; All-powerful and Wise; inflicting evil; forgiving sins; the guardian of Immortality. Varuna is often regarded as the Supreme Deity.

Vayu (Zor.) The Wind-God.

Vedas (Hin.) The name of the four works which constitute the Hindu sacred scriptures. The four works are:
Atharva-Veda: deals with magical charms, spells, incantations and kingly duties
Sama-Veda: stanzas from the Rig-Veda, arranged for various sacrifices
Yajur-Veda: sacrificial prayers and verses from the Rig-Veda
Rig-Veda: contains a collection of 1017 chants of prayer and praise addressed to a number of gods.
Attached to the Vedas are the Brahmanas and the Upanishads.

Videvdat (Zor.) The third group of writings in the Zoroastrian scriptures. (See also *Avesta*)

Vinaya (Bud.) See *Tripitaka*.

Vishnu (Hin.) The second god in the Hindu Triad. (See also *Hindu Triad*)

Vispered (Zor.) A collection of liturgical work assembled in the Avesta.

Vivahvant (Zor.) The Sky-God.

Vohu Mana (Zor.) Good Mind; the first of the six Zoroastrian Divine Powers.

Yajur-Veda (Hin.) See *Vedas*.

Yasht (Zor.) The second group of writings in the Zoroastrian scriptures. (See also *Avesta*)

Yasna (Zor.) The first group of writings in the Zoroastrian scriptures. (See also *Avesta*)

Yima (Zor.) The Death-God.

Yoga (Hin.) The term means "yoke" or "joining" in the sense of that which unites.

Yom Kippur (Jud.) The Day of Atonement, which falls ten days after the Jewish New Year (Rosh Hashanah). This is one of the most solemn religious days and is devoted to soul-searching, confession of sins, and repentance.

Zakat (Isl.) Almsgiving, charity.

Zamzam (Isl.) Name of the sacred well next to the Ka'aba shrine in Mecca, where Hagar and Ishamel stopped for water.

Zazen (Bud.) A part of Zen Buddhist training involved in sitting in meditation.

Zealots (Jud.) A term currently used to designate the more radical and warlike Jewish group opposed to foreign rule. Previously, the term was applied to those who kept the laws meticulously, and who carefully guarded the institutions of their forefathers.

Zen (Bud.) Meditation; the equivalent to the Chinese term "Ch'an".

Bibliography

Sacred Scriptures and Anthologies

Adler, M. *The World of the Talmud*. New York: Schocken Books, 1970.

Arberry, A.J. *The Koran Interpreted*. London: Oxford University Press, 1964.

Ballou, R.O. *World Bible*. New York: The Viking Press, 1967.

Bode, D.F.A., and Nanavutty, P. *Songs of Zarathustra*. London: George Allen & Unwin, 1952.

Bouquet, A.C. *Sacred Books of the World*. London: Penguin Books, 1967.

Browne, L. *The World's Great Scriptures*. New York: The Macmillan Co., 1946.

Burtt, E.A., ed. *Teachings of the Compassionate Buddha*. New York: New American Library, 1955.

Champion, S.G., and Short, D. *Readings from World Religions*. New York: Fawcett Publishers, 1959.

Cohen, A. *Everyman's Talmud*. New York: E.P. Dutton, 1949.

Conze, E. *Buddhist Scriptures*. London: Penguin Books, 1959.

Duchesne-Guillemin, J. *The Hymns of Zoroaster*. Boston: Beacon Press, 1963.

Edgerton, E., trans. *The Bhagavad-Gita*. New York: Harper & Row, 1968.

Gaer, J. *What the Great Religions Believe*. New York: New American Library, 1963.

Lanczkowski, G. *Sacred Writings: A Guide to the Literature of Religions*. London: Wm. Collins, 1961.

Nikhilananda, S., trans. *The Uphanishads*. New York: Harper & Row, 1964.

Pickthall, M.W., trans. *The Meaning of the Glorious Koran*. New York: New American Library, 1953.

Warren, H.C. *Buddhism in Translations*. New York: Atheneum Publishers, 1963.

Zaehner, R.C., ed. *Hindu Scriptures*. London: Dent, 1966.

General

Adams, C.J., ed. *A Reader's Guide to the Great Religions*. New York: Free Press, 1965.

Aletrino, L. *Six World Religions*. London: SCM Press, 1968.

Bouquet, A.C. *Comparative Religion: A Short Outline*. London: Penguin Books, 1969.

Bradley, D.G. *A Guide to the World's Religions*. New Jersey: Prentice-Hall, 1963.

Denney, A. *World Faiths and Modern Problems*. London: Hamilton, Hamish, 1969.

Finegan, J. *The Archaeology of World Religions*. Princeton: Princeton University Press, 1966.

Gaer, J. *How the Great Religions Began.* New York: Dodd, Mead & Co., 1956.
Hilliard, F.H. *How Men Worship.* London: Routledge & Kegan Paul, 1969.
Landis, B.Y. *World Religions.* rev. ed. Toronto: Clarke, Irwin & Co., 1971.
Lewis, H.D., and Slater, R.L. *The Study of Religions: Meeting Points and Major Issues.* Baltimore: Penguin Books, 1969.
Ling, T.O. *A History of Religion: East and West; An Introduction and Interpretation.* London: Macmillan & Co., 1969.
Noss, J.B. *Man's Religions.* 4th ed. New York: The Macmillan Co., 1970.
Parrinder, E.G. *The World's Living Religions.* London: Pan Books, 1969.
―――. *What World Religions Teach.* 2d ed. London: George G. Harrap & Co., 1968.
―――. *Worship in the World's Religions.* London: Faber & Faber, 1961.
Potter, C.F. *Great Religious Leaders.* New York: Simon & Schuster, 1958.
Slater, R.L. *World Religions and World Community.* New York: Columbia University Press, 1963.
Smart, N. *The Religious Experience of Mankind.* New York: Charles Scribner's Sons, 1969.
―――. *World Religions: A Dialogue.* Baltimore: Penguin, 1966.
Smith, H. *The Religions of Man.* New York: Harper & Row, 1958.
Tillich, P.J. *Christianity and the Encounter of the World Religions.* New York: Columbia University Press, 1963.
Toynbee, A.J. *Christianity Among the Religions of the World.* New York: Charles Scribner's Sons, 1957.
Van Leeuwen, A. *Christianity in World History.* New York: Charles Scribner's Sons, 1964.
Voss, C.H. *In Search of Meaning: Living Religions of the World.* New York: The World Publishing Co., Excalibur, 1968.
Zachner, R.C., ed. *The Concise Encyclopedia of Living Faiths.* Boston: Beacon Press, 1959.

Judaism

Baeck, L. *The Essence of Judaism.* rev. ed. New York: Schocken Books Inc., 1961.
Belford, L. *Introduction to Judaism.* New York: Association Press, 1970.
Bentwich, N. *The Jews in Our Time.* Baltimore: Penguin Books.
Blau, J.L. *Modern Varieties of Judaism.* New York: Columbia University Press, 1966.
Domnitz, M. *Judaism.* London: Ward, Lock & Co., 1970.
Epstein, I. *Judaism: An Historical Presentation.* Baltimore: Penguin Books, 1968.
Fackenheim, E.L. *Paths to Jewish Belief.* New York: Behrman House.
Fishman, I. *Introduction to Judaism.* London: Vallentine, Mitchell & Co., 1964.
Goodman, P. *History of the Jews.* Revised by I. Cohen. New York: E.P. Dutton & Co., Everyman.
Herberg, W. *Judaism and Modern Man.* New York: Atheneum Publishers, 1970.
Isserman, F.M. *This Is Judaism.* Chicago: Willet, Clark & Co., 1944.
Jacobs, L. *Principles of the Jewish Faith.* London: Vallentine, Mitchell & Co., 1964.
Kaufmann, Y. *The Religion of Israel.* Abridged and translated by M. Greenberg. Chicago: University of Chicago Press, 1960.
Neusner, J. *The Way of the Torah: An Introduction to Judaism.* Belmont, Calif.: Dickenson Publishing Co., 1970.
Schector, S. *Studies in Judaism.* New York: The World Publishing Co., Meridian Books.
Scholem, G.G. *Major Trends in Jewish Mysticism.* New York: Schocken Books, 1946.
Simon, M. *Jewish Religious Conflicts.* London: Hutchinson & Co., 1950.
Simpson, W.W. *Jewish Prayer and Worship.* London: SCM Press, 1965.

Christianity

Anderson, B.W. *The Unfolding Drama of the Bible.* New York: Association Press.
Bainton, R.H. *Early Christianity.* Princeton, N.J.: D. Van Nostrand Co., Anvil, 1960.
―――, et al. *Horizon History of Christianity.* New York: Harper & Row, 1964.
―――. *The Reformation of the Sixteenth Century.* Boston: Beacon Press, 1962.

Benz, E. *The Eastern Orthodox Church: Its Thought and Life.* New York: Doubleday & Co., 1963.

Bultman, R. *Primitive Christianity in Its Contemporary Setting.* New York: The World Publishing Co., Meridian, 1956.

Chery, A. *What Is the Mass.* Westminster, Md.: The Newman Press, 1952.

Constantelos, D.J. *Greek Orthodox Church: Faith, History and Practice.* New York: Seabury Press, 1967.

Cook, S. *Introduction to the Bible.* Baltimore: Penguin.

Corbett, J.A. *The Papacy: A Brief History.* Princeton, N.J.: D. Van Nostrand Co., Anvil.

Craig, C.T. *The Beginning of Christianity.* New York: Abingdon Press.

Dunstan, T.L., ed. *Protestantism.* New York: Washington Square Press, 1967.

Every, G. *Christian Mythology.* London: Hamlyn Publishing Group, 1970.

French, R.M. *The Eastern Orthodox Church.* London: Hutchinson, 1951.

Goodspeed, E.J. *How Came the Bible.* New York: Abingdon Press.

————. *The Life of Jesus.* New York: Harper & Bros. 1950.

Hofstatter, H.H. *Art of the Late Middle Ages.* New York: Harry N. Abrams, 1968.

Hughes, P. *Popular History of the Catholic Church.* New York: Doubleday Image Books.

Livingstone, J.C. *Modern Christian Thought: From the Enlightenment to Vatican II.* New York: The Macmillan Co., 1971.

Lossky, V. *The Mystical Theology of the Eastern Church.* London: James Clarke, 1957.

McKenzie, J.L. *The Roman Catholic Church.* London: Holt, Rinehart & Winston, 1969.

Schmemann, A. *The Historical Road of Eastern Orthodoxy.* Chicago: Henry Regnery Co., 1966.

Stuber, S.I. *Denominations: How We Got Them.* New York: Associated Press, 1958.

Weiser, F.X. *Handbook of Christian Feasts and Customs.* New Jersey: Paulist Press, 1958.

Islam

'Ali, M. *The Religion of Islam.* Lahore, India, 1950.

'Ali, S.A. *The Spirit of Islam.* London: Christopher's, 1922.

Andrae, T. *Mohammed: The Man and His Faith.* New York: Harper & Bros., 1960.

Arberry, A.J. *Sufism.* London: George Allen & Unwin, 1950.

————. *Reason and Revelation in Islam.* London: George Allen & Unwin, 1957.

Arnold, T.W. *The Teaching of Islam.* London: Luzac & Co., 1956.

Atiyah, E. *The Arabs.* London: Penguin.

Bell, R. *Introduction to the Qur'an.* Edinburgh: Edinburgh University Press, 1953.

Bodley, R.V.C. *The Messenger: The Life of Mohammed.* New York: Doubleday & Co., 1946.

Calverley, E.E. *Worship in Islam.* London: Luzac & Co., 1957.

Cragg, K. *The Call of the Minaret.* Oxford: Oxford University Press, 1956.

————. *The House of Islam.* New Jersey: Prentice-Hall, 1969.

Dermenghem, E. *Muhammad and the Islamic Tradition.* New York: Harper & Bros., Men of Wisdom Series, 6.

Donaldson, D.M. *The Shi'ite Religion.* London: Luzac & Co., 1933.

Gaudefoy-Demombynes, M. *Muslim Institutions.* New York: The Macmillan Co., 1951.

Gibb, H.A.R. *Mohammedanism: An Historical Survey.* Oxford: Oxford University Press, 1949.

Grube, E.J. *The World of Islam.* London: Hamlyn Publishing Group, 1967.

Grunebaum, von, G.E. *Medieval Islam.* Chicago: University of Chicago Press, 1953.

Guillaume, A. *Islam.* New York: Penguin, 1969.

————. *Life of Muhammed.* Oxford: Oxford University Press, 1955.

Hollister, J.N. *The Shia of India.* London: Luzac & Co., 1953.

Nicholson, R.A. *Studies in Islamic Mysticism.* Cambridge: Cambridge University Press, 1921.

Smith, W.C. *Islam in Modern History.* New York: New American Library, 1959.

Sugana, G.M. *The Life and Times of Muhammad.* London: Hamlyn Publishing Group, 1969.

Watt, W.M. *Muhammed: Prophet and Statesman*. London: Oxford University Press, 1961.
———. *Free Will and Predestination in Early Islam*. London: Luzac & Co., 1948.

Hinduism
Appasamy, A.J. *Temple Bells*. London: SCM Press, 1930.
Archer, W.G. *The Loves of Krishna*. New York: Grove Press.
Ashe, G. *Ghandi: A Study in Revolution*. London: Wm. Heinemann, 1968.
Bahm, A.J. *Yoga: Union with the Ultimate*. New York: Frederick Unger Publishing Co.
Basham, A.L. *The Wonder That Was India*. 3rd ed. New York: Taplinger Publishing Co., 1968.
Behnan, K.T. *Yoga*. New York: Dover Publishers, 1960.
Bouquet, A.C. *Hinduism*. 2d ed. New York: Hutchinson University Library, 1966.
Coomaraswamy, A.K. *The Dance of Shiva*. rev. ed. New York: The Noonday Press.
Dasgupta, S.N. *Yoga as Philosophy and Religion*. London: Kegan Paul, Trench, Trubner & Co., 1924.
———. *Hindu Mysticism*. La Salle, Ind.: Open Court Publishing Co., 1927.
Edwards, M. *Indian Temples and Palaces*. London: Hamlyn Publishing Group, 1969.
Gandhi, M. *An Autobiography: Or The Story of My Experiments with Truth*. Translated by M. Desai. Boston: Beacon Press, 1959.
Ghurye, G.S. *Caste and Class in India*. 2d ed. Bombay: Popular Book Depot, 1957.
———. *Indian Sadhus*. Bombay: Popular Book Depot, 1953.
Hopkins, T.J. *The Hindu Religious Tradition*. Belmont, Calif.: Dickenson Publishing Co., 1971.
Ions, V. *Indian Mythology*. London: Hamlyn Publishing Group, 1967.
Kramrisch, S. *The Art of India Through the Ages*. 3rd ed. New York: Praeger Publishers, 1965.
Lewis, O. *Village Life in North India*. Urbana, Ill.: University of Illinois Press, 1958.
Narayan, R.K. *Gods, Demons and Others*. London: Wm. Heinemann, 1965.
Pitt, M. *Introducing Hinduism*. New York: Friendship Press.
Radhakrishnan, S. *The Hindu View of Life*. London: George Allen & Unwin, 1960.
Renou, L. *Religions of Ancient India*. Oxford: Oxford University Press, 1953.
Singer, M., ed. *Krishna; Myths, Rites and Attitudes*. Chicago: Chicago University Press, 1969.
Smart, N. *The Yogi and the Devotee*. London: George Allen & Unwin, 1968.
Thomas, P. *Hindu Religions, Customs and Manners*. London: Luzac & Co., 1956.
Walker, B. *Hindu World: An Encyclopaedic Survey of Hinduism*. London: George Allen & Unwin, 1968.
Wood, E. *Yoga*. New York: Penguin, 1970.
Zaehner, R.C. *Hinduism*. London: Oxford University Press, 1962.
Zimmer, H. *Myth and Symbol in Indian Art and Civilization*. New York: Harper Torchbook, 1962.

Buddhism
Allen, G.F. *The Buddha's Philosophy*. London: Macmillan & Co., 1959.
Anesaki, M. *The History of Japanese Religion*. London: Kegan Paul, Trench, Trubner & Co., 1931.
Arnold, E. *The Light of Asia. The Life and Teaching of Gautama*. New York: Dolphin Books.
Aspinwall, M. *Jataka Tales Out of Old India*. New York: G.P. Putnam's Sons, 1927.
Aung, M.T. *Folk Elements in Burmese Buddhism*. London: Oxford University Press, 1962.
Bahm, A.J. *The Philosophy of the Buddha*. New York: Collier Books.
Bell, C. *The Religion of Tibet*. New York: Oxford University Press, 1931.
Branen, N.S. *Soka Gakkai: Japan's Militant Buddhist*. Richmond, Va.: John Know Press, 1970.
Brewster, E.H. *Life of Gotama the Buddha*. London: K. Paul, Trench, Trubner, 1926.
Ch'en, K.K.S. *Buddhism in China*. Princeton: Princeton University Press, 1964.

Conze, E. *Buddhism: Its Essence and Development*. New York: Harper & Row, 1959.
———. *A Short History of Buddhism*. Bombay: Chentana, 1960.
———. *Buddhist Thought in India*. London: George Allen & Unwin, 1962.
Coomaraswamy, A.K. *Buddha and the Gospel of Buddhism*. New York: Harper & Row, 1966.
Dasgupta, S.B. *An Introduction to Tantric Buddhism*. 2d ed. Calcutta: University of Calcutta, 1958.
Dhaninivat, K.B. *A History of Buddhism in Siam*. Bangkok: The Siam Society, 1960.
Dutt, S., *Buddhist Monks and Monasteries of India*. London: George Allen & Unwin, 1963.
Evans-Wentz, W.Y., ed. *The Tibetan Book of the Great Liberation*. New York: Oxford University Press, 1954.
Gard, R.A., ed. *Buddhism*. New York: Washington Square Press, 1969.
Glassenap, H. von. *Buddhism: A Non-Theistic Religion*. London: George Allen & Unwin, 1970.
Hilliard, F.H. *The Buddha, The Prophet, and The Christ*. New York: The Macmillan Co., 1956.
Hilska, V. *Great Architecture of Japan*. London: Hamlyn Publishing Group.
———. *Buddhism*. Baltimore: Penguin, 1962.
Jennings, J.G. *The Vedantic Buddhism of the Buddha*. Oxford: Oxford University Press, 1948.
Keith, A.B. *Buddhist Philosophy in India and Ceylon*. New York: Oxford University Press, 1923.
Kitagawa, J.M. *Religion in Japanese History*. New York: Columbia University Press, 1966.
Legett, T.P. *A First Zen Reader*. Ruthland, Vt.: Charles E. Tuttle Co., 1960.
Ling, T.O. *Buddhism and the Mythology of Evil*. London: George Allen & Unwin, 1962.
———. *Buddha, Marx and God*. New York: The Macmillan Co., 1966.
Morgan, K.W., ed. *The Path of Buddhism*. New York: Ronald Press, 1956.
Rahula, W. *What the Buddha Taught*. New York: Grove Press, 1962.
Reichelt, K.L. *Religion in Chinese Garment*. New York: Philosophical Library, 1952.
Richardson, H.E. *Tibet and Its History*. Oxford: Oxford University Press, 1962.
Robinson, R.H. *Buddhist Religion: An Historical Introduction*. Belmont, Calif.: Dickenson Publishing Co., 1970.
Shangharakshita, B. *The Three Jewels: An Introduction to Buddhism*. London: Hutchinson Publishing Group, 1968.
Sugana, G.M. *The Life and Times of Buddha*. London: Hamlyn Publishing Group, 1969.
Suzuki, B.L. *Mahayana Buddhism*. London: George Allen & Unwin, 1959.
Suzuki, D.T. *The Essence of Buddhism*. London: Luzac & Co., 1957.
———. *Studies in Zen*. New York: Dell Publishing Co., 1955.
———. *The Training of the Zen Buddhist Monk*. Kyoto: The Eastern Buddhist Society, 1934.
Thomas, E.J. *The Life of Buddha as Legend and History*. 3rd ed. London: Kegan Paul, Trench, Trubner, 1949.
Watts, A.W. *The Way of Zen*. Baltimore: Penguin, 1968.
Wright, A.F. *Buddhism in Chinese History*. New York: Athenium, 1967.
Zimmer, H. *Philosophies of India*. Princeton: Princeton University Press, 1969.

Zoroastrianism

Dhalla, M.N. *History of Zoroastrianism*. Oxford: Oxford University Press, 1938.
Duchesne-Guillemin, J. *The Western Response to Zoroaster*. Oxford: Oxford University Press, 1958.
———. *Zoroastrianism Symbols and Values*. New York: Harper & Row. 1970.
Frye, R.N. *The Heritage of Persia*. Toronto: Mentor, 1966.
Gersheyitch, I. *The Avestan Hymn to Mithra*. Cambridge: Cambridge University Press, 1959.
Ghirshman, R. *Iran*. Baltimore: Penguin Books, 1954.

Henning W.B. *Zoroaster: Politician or Witch Doctor?* Oxford: Oxford University Press, 1950.

Herzfeld, E. *Zoroaster and His World*. 2 vols. Princeton: Princeton University Press, 1947.

Hinnells, J.R. *Persian Mythology*. London: Hamlyn Publishing Group, 1971.

Jackson, A.V.W. *Zoroaster: The Prophet of Ancient Iran*. New York: Columbia University Press, 1898.

———. *Zoroastrian Studies*. New York: Columbia University Press, 1928.

Masani, R. *The Religion of the Good Life*. London: George Allen & Unwin, 1938.

Modi, J.J. *Religious Ceremonies and Customs of the Parsis*. 2d ed. London: Luzac & Co., 1954.

Moulton, J.H. *The Treasure of the Magi*. Oxford: Oxford University Press, 1917.

Pavry, J.D.C. *The Zoroastrian Doctrine of the Future Life*. New York: Columbia University Press, 1926.

Zaehner, R.C. *The Teachings of the Magi*. London: George Allen & Unwin, 1956.

———. *The Dawn and Twilight of Zoroastrianism*. New York: G.P. Putnam & Sons, 1961.

Index